LOVE
BUSTERS

Other books by Willard F. Harley, Jr.

His Needs, Her Needs
Five Steps to Romantic Love
Give and Take

LOVE BUSTERS

*Overcoming the Habits
That Destroy Romantic Love*

Second Edition

Willard F. Harley, Jr.

Fleming H. Revell
A Division of Baker Book House Co
Grand Rapids, Michigan 49516

Some of the material in this book and its basic principles previously appeared in *Marriage Insurance* by Willard F. Harley, Jr.

Copyright © 1992, 1997 by Willard F. Harley, Jr.
Published by Fleming H. Revell
a division of Baker Book House Company
P.O. Box 6287, Grand Rapids, MI 49516-6287

Fourth printing, February 2000

Printed in the United States of America

Library of Congress Cataloging-in-Publication Data

Harley, Willard F.
   Love busters / Willard F. Harley, Jr.—2nd ed.
      p.   cm.
   ISBN 0-8007-1739-2 (cloth)
    1. Marriage. 2. Communication in marriage. 3. Man-woman
relationships. I. Title.
HQ734.H284   1997
646.7'8—dc21   97-1794

For information about academic books, resources for Christian leaders, and all new releases available from Baker Book House, visit our web site:
http://www.bakerbooks.com

To
Joyce

The love of my life

Contents

Introduction

When a man and woman get married, they think their feelings of romantic love will last a lifetime. The vows and commitments they make usually depend on that assumption.

But romantic love, that feeling of incredible attraction, is short-lived for most couples. Many sustain it for just a few months or years after the wedding. For others, it's only days. And when it goes, the commitments of marriage usually go with it.

Some marriage counselors advise couples to accept the inevitable: Enjoy romantic love while it lasts but don't expect it to continue forever. Some recommend rising to a higher form of passionless love, while others suggest divorce.

But I believe that couples don't have to accept the loss of romantic love as inevitable. Instead, they can *restore* the romantic love they once had for each other. Once it's back, all thoughts of divorce or passionless love vanish.

Impossible, you may say. It may certainly seem that way. When you're in love, it seems impossible that you will ever lose that feeling; and when you're "out of love," it seems impossible to get it back. Most couples I counsel don't believe they will ever feel that love for each other again. But my methods do not require faith—they require action! When a couple follows my instructions, their love usually returns, ending the threat of divorce.

During courtship, a man and woman create the feeling of romantic love for each other by meeting each other's most important emotional needs. But after they get married, they develop habits that destroy their love for each other. I call those destructive habits Love Busters. As long as Love Busters are tolerated, romantic love doesn't have a chance.

The lessons of this book will teach you how to throw the rascals out. I identify the five most common Love Busters and explain how couples have learned to overcome them. Once they're gone, romantic love has free rein in marriage.

This book and its companion, *His Needs, Her Needs,* work together in helping couples build and sustain romantic love. While *Love Busters* will help you avoid *losing* romantic love, *His Needs, Her Needs* will help you *build* romantic love by teaching you how to meet each other's most important emotional needs.

The assignments suggested in both of these books require the use of forms I've created over the years. But due to space and size limitations in these books, I've printed them in a larger and more convenient format in the workbook *Five Steps to Romantic Love: A Workbook for Readers of* Love Busters *and* His Needs, Her Needs. I recommend it to you as a supplement to this book.

The feeling of love that you and your spouse share is an essential part of your marriage. Without it, your marriage is likely to fail. You must not downplay its importance.

But if you have lost that feeling of love toward each other, don't despair. Romantic love can be restored if you follow my advice. And once you get it back, you'll agree that it's much too valuable to ever lose again.

How Love Busters 1
Can Wreck a Marriage

Karen couldn't remember what it was like being in love with Jim. Whenever he was home, her stomach knotted up and she often felt sick. When they talked, which wasn't very often, she was usually on the defensive. Vacationing together was unthinkable—if she wanted to relax, he had to be far away. Could she survive this marriage long enough for her children to grow up? It was looking increasingly hopeless to her.

When I talked with Karen for the first time, she wanted a separation from Jim, one that would help her survive a few more years of their marriage. Their youngest daughter, Lisa, was thirteen. For Lisa's sake, Karen wanted to wait five or six years to divorce Jim.

You may not be feeling as desperate as Karen felt that day but perhaps you know what she was going through—the fighting, the sarcasm, the disrespect and . . . the loneliness. But marriage is supposed to be different, isn't it? It should be a caring relationship, where a husband and wife treat each other with kindness and consideration, not with rudeness and anger.

Karen had expected her marriage to be perfect. Within a month of their first date, she was madly in love with Jim. He seemed too good to be true—attractive and intelligent and he shared most of her values.

What impressed her the most was his thoughtfulness. He eagerly helped her whenever she had a problem; he changed his plans whenever they conflicted with hers; and he was never argumentative, always willing to see things from her perspective. Again and again Jim proved to Karen that caring for her was his highest priority—and that made her feel very secure.

Jim had been in love with Karen too. From the beginning of their relationship, she had made him feel special. She found him fascinating to talk to and showered him with affection and admiration. He had never known a woman as beautiful as Karen, and—miracle of miracles—she *loved* him! This was the woman he wanted for life; she seemed perfect in every way. Within a year they were married.

Jim's Neglect

It wasn't long after the wedding that Jim felt the financial pressure of being a family man. Karen was pregnant within the first year of their marriage and she planned to work fewer hours after their child arrived. Jim figured his income had to increase to make up the difference, so he decided to work longer hours to advance his career.

With more of his time and energy spent at work, Jim's thoughtfulness eroded. Instead of jumping to solve Karen's problems, he now expected her to work things out on her own. Instead of changing his plans to help her, he insisted that Karen rearrange her schedule to accommodate his. *After all,* he thought, *we're both intelligent adults. She can take the car to the garage just as easily as I can. Why should she expect me to drop everything at work to do something she can do for herself? Am I her slave? Is she a princess?*

At first, Karen was deeply troubled by his change of attitude, though she tried not to show it. She made a valiant effort to accommodate him, troubleshooting around the home, rearranging her schedule to fit his, but when she was alone, she cried. *Why had he changed so much?*

Over time, Karen's conviction that Jim cared for her was seriously damaged. He was no longer meeting her needs; that's for sure. She felt he had cut her loose to fend for herself. *Maybe,* she thought, *he no longer loves me.* As the chemistry of their relationship deteriorated, her care for him deteriorated with it. In response to Jim's neglect of her, Karen began to neglect him. She no longer asked him how his day went. She was not showing much affection or admiration anymore. And she wasn't very enthusiastic about making love either.

When Jim began to neglect Karen, something strange happened to his appearance—at least the way he appeared to her. He just wasn't as attractive to her as he had once been. He *had* gained ten pounds, so maybe his loss of body tone was the problem. *If he'd firm up a little, I'd find him more attractive,* she thought. But when he lost the weight and worked out a little more often, it didn't help.

Karen's Loss of Sexual Interest

Jim didn't pay much attention to the fact that Karen had stopped being affectionate or that she wasn't as admiring. But he sure noticed her loss of sexual interest. When they were first married, she had looked forward to making love to Jim, but now it was something she tried to avoid. Whenever they made love, she felt used.

One day Jim got up the courage to ask her what was going on. "Karen, what's happening to you? Why aren't you interested in making love anymore?"

"I'm sorry, Jim," she replied. "I just haven't been in the mood lately. I don't know why."

That was not an honest answer. She knew she was withdrawing from sex because she felt abandoned by Jim, but she didn't think there would be any point in discussing it.

And what could he say? She just wasn't in the mood—or so she said.

"What do you think it would take to get you in the mood?" It was difficult for Jim to raise the subject. He felt like he was begging.

But Karen wasn't making it easy for him, either. "I don't know," she answered. "I've never given it much thought."

The truth was Jim had stopped meeting some of Karen's most important emotional needs. He was not as affectionate, not as supportive, not as accommodating, and he certainly didn't spend as much quality time with her. Consequently, she was not as motivated to meet his needs. Sex, it turned out, was something she felt like doing only when she knew that Jim loved and cared for her. Now she was feeling emotionally abandoned, so what had formerly been effortless became difficult.

Throughout their marriage, they had rarely shared their innermost feelings with each other. When one offended the other, the problem was usually shrugged off—they never really negotiated solutions. But now they had a problem they could not shrug off. Jim didn't want to go through life with a sexually reluctant wife. Karen didn't know how to tell him what was bothering her, and part of it she didn't understand herself.

Karen's feelings of sexual attraction toward her husband were very fragile and without those feelings she was not comfortable making love. Jim learned this the hard way. But what he learned didn't help him understand the problem. He still didn't realize that it was his failure to meet her emotional needs that changed her feelings.

At this point, if Jim had understood the problem, he could have fixed it rather easily. If Jim had recognized that his failure to meet Karen's emotional needs had taken its toll on his sexual attractiveness, he could have simply gone back to meeting her needs, doing what had drawn them together in the beginning. He could have cheerfully kept her car repaired and accommodated her in his schedule. *Presto,* sexual problem solved!

But Jim didn't understand the problem nor how to solve it. And his frustration introduced a new and destructive chapter in their marriage. He had a choice. He could solve his sexual problem with care and understanding or he could try selfish demands. Regretfully, he chose the latter.

One night, after Jim and Karen had gone to bed, he reached over to kiss her goodnight. Thinking he was interested in making love, she pushed him away. Jim's feelings of resentment had been building for some time and her rejection pushed him over the edge. He was furious. Throwing her out of bed, he called her names and lectured her for half an hour about her bad attitude. All his resentment poured out in a moment of unrestrained rage.

Karen huddled in a corner, afraid he would hit her. She didn't dare say a word. Eventually he settled down.

When it was over, Jim felt much better. He had finally said what he had felt for such a long time. But Karen was a basket case. He started to apologize for losing his temper but then stopped himself. *I'm glad I had the courage to say what I felt,* he thought. *Now we're getting somewhere!*

The Road to Marital Disaster

They were getting somewhere all right but not where Jim thought. They were now on the road to marital disaster.

Jim put his arm around Karen, telling her how much he loved her. Still in the corner, she didn't dare push him away now. All she could do was cry. As he became more amorous, she let him do anything he wanted—eventually they made love. Jim felt it was one of their best sexual experiences ever. Karen felt raped.

Many women would have gone straight to an attorney the next day to end the marriage, but Karen believed she had married Jim for life. So the next day, when she had time to reflect on the nightmare she had experienced, she made some decisions that she thought would help her survive.

First, she would never be found cowering in a corner again. Next time he lost his temper, she would fight fire with fire—let him know what a creep she thought he had become.

Second, because Jim got what he wanted by forcing her, she would get what she wanted by forcing him. In the past, when she needed something from him and he refused, she would do it herself. Now she would not accept no for an answer. She would *demand* what she wanted.

Third, she would learn to emotionally distance herself from Jim. He hadn't hit her that fateful night but he hurt her deeply—emotionally. She would remain married to him but never again become emotionally vulnerable to him. She needed to create a life of her own that was completely separate from his.

She made one huge concession, however. What made him so angry was his unmet need for sex, so anytime he wanted sex, she obliged. Deep down, she felt it was her responsibility. She would even try to enjoy it but she knew their relationship would never be the same.

At first, Jim thought his prayers had been answered. Whenever he wanted sex, he got it. And Karen was noticeably more passionate. For the first week they made love every night.

But the rest of their relationship was going downhill fast. Jim didn't make any changes in his behavior to meet Karen's needs. He was still expecting her to do things for herself, and that fit quite nicely into her new agenda. She didn't *want* him to meet her emotional needs anymore.

Karen began to demand that Jim meet her nonemotional needs—getting the car repaired, adjusting his schedule to hers. Her demands caught him off guard, but he grudgingly obliged. Yet, since she had to force him to do these things, he got no credit for meeting her needs and he was not becoming any more attractive to her.

As she had planned, Karen developed a weekly schedule that did not include Jim. Off to work by 6:00 A.M., she'd get home as late as 10:00 P.M. Weekends were spent with her friends. The money she earned went into her own separate account and she made Jim pay as many of the bills as she could.

Despite all this distancing behavior, she stayed true to her decision to give Jim the sex he wanted—at least at first.

Though Jim now had no sexual complaints, he was still angry much of the time. He was particularly upset with Karen's failure to let him know where she was going or what she had been doing. Whenever he asked, she told him it was none of his business. When he argued with her about her secrecy, she would scream at him to leave her alone. Then she would threaten to leave him. Once she even threw things at him.

I suppose Jim would have been willing to suffer through the bad marriage for the rest of his life if Karen had made love to him every night, but, as it turns out, her commitment only lasted a few weeks. At first, she allowed herself to say no once in a while, but within a few months she was saying no almost all the time.

Actually, her commitment was poorly conceived. None of us can force ourselves to do something unpleasant indefinitely. Sooner or later we all find excuses to avoid it. There's hardly a woman anywhere who can consistently make love to a husband she dislikes. And Karen was getting to hate hers. Within a few months, Karen couldn't make love to Jim anymore. Her stomach knotted up at the very thought of it.

The brief reprieve that had been brought on by frequent love-making came to an end. Jim and Karen were left with their independent lifestyles, demands, anger, disrespect, and dishonesty. No marriage can last very long with those weights dragging it down.

By the time they made their first appointment with me, they were not meeting any of each other's emotional needs. But what's worse, they were deliberately hurting each other. They could hardly remember what it was like being in love.

The Choice

Jim and Karen's experience is all too common in today's marriages. What starts out as a caring and thoughtful relationship often disintegrates into thoughtlessness. As a husband and wife stop meeting each other's needs and start hurting each other, love turns into hate.

Some couples suffer through years of lovelessness for the sake of their children or their religious convictions. But all too often, they try to get off the train of their marriage—they file for divorce.

Unfortunately, the train doesn't stop. It's rushing forward at a high speed, and the exit is usually a disaster for the couple and their family.

Since so much personal and familial happiness depends on the success of marriage, you'd think that couples would approach it with a careful plan to insure success. But sadly, most don't give their marriages much thought until it's almost too late. About half of all marriages end in divorce, and most of the others are a disappointment. Very few marriages turn out to be as happy as they could have been.

I'd like your marriage to be one of the exceptions. I've written this book to help you build a happy marriage that *stays* happy. If you follow my advice, you're likely to enjoy a lifetime of love. My recommendations have helped thousands of people turn from marital pain to marital pleasure, and you can be one of them.

The principles I advocate are not revolutionary—in fact, they're somewhat traditional. But in a century where people have been noted for their increasing self-centeredness, caring more for their own interests than those of others (particularly their spouse), these principles have been forgotten.

You don't have to be the victim of recent social trends. Instead you can choose a course for your family that will make you the happy exception.

The Love Bank

How can we explain the rise and fall of Jim and Karen's marriage? Let me introduce you to the **Love Bank**. It's a concept I developed to help those I counsel understand how the feelings of love are created and destroyed.

We're all born with a Love Bank. The people we meet are automatically assigned their own "accounts," and every experience we have with them affects the balances of love units in their accounts. All this goes on inside us throughout our lives, twenty-four hours a day.

When we associate good feelings with people, love units are deposited into their accounts. Bad feelings cause love units to be withdrawn.

Most of the time, our feelings are neutral, neither good nor bad, so people's accounts don't change much. But once in a while, our feelings are so good or so bad that huge deposits or withdrawals can take place at a single encounter.

When people have high balances of love units in their accounts with us, we *like* them. We associate them with the good experiences we have had with them. But once in a while, someone of the opposite sex meets our most important emotional needs. When that happens, so many love units are deposited that his or her account hits a threshold and we *fall in love*. That's what I call the feeling of *romantic love*.

People can have balances with us that are in the red. They withdraw more love units than they deposit. We *dislike* those people because they are associated with bad experiences. And when someone's balance is very much in the red, we *hate* that person.

Most of our relationships are voluntary. That is, we choose which people we'll spend our time with. Naturally we tend to choose those who have deposited love units in our Love Bank, so that they will keep depositing them. In this way, we come to like these people more and more.

On the other hand, if someone starts withdrawing love units, we begin to avoid that person if we can. We usually don't give such people a chance to withdraw very many love units, so we seldom get to a point where we dislike them strongly or hate them. We "close their account" before things get that bad.

But many relationships are not voluntary. At work, at home, in our churches, clubs, or community activities, we have to deal with certain people whether we like them or not. These are the people we can grow to hate, because we can't easily get away from them as they continue to withdraw love units.

If things get too bad, you could find another job or switch churches, but a family is a different story. It is difficult to avoid uncles and aunts, cousins, and other close relatives—but it can be done if they're obnoxious enough. With even greater effort it is possible to avoid parents and children. But a spouse is almost impossible to avoid, as long as you're still married. So it should come as no surprise that the person you are most likely to hate is your spouse because that's the person you can't get away from—no matter how miserable he or she makes you.

Day after day, month after month, year after year, your spouse can withdraw love units by criticizing you, lying to you, making demands of you, annoying you with disgusting habits and thought-less activities, calling you disrespectful names, and even being phys-ically or verbally abusive to you. And what can you do about it? You can't get away. That would mean a divorce or at least a separation. What can you do to get him or her to stop? You do what most people do: Dish it back as fast as it comes. If you're going to be miserable, then, by golly, you're *both* going to be miserable.

When a married couple's relationship starts on a downward slide, the love loss actually gains momentum. Love units are withdrawn in ever increasing numbers, because every action—even an innocent one—is seen as uncaring and insensitive. Because they live together, a couple cannot avoid each other, and withdrawals continue unabated. The end result is often the violence that comes from a deep and pervasive hatred.

I have counseled both victims and perpetrators of domestic vio-lence, and the difference between them is often only a matter of strength and opportunity. In many cases, their roles are reversed when the perpetrator becomes weak. They both hate and want to hurt each other. The sad fact is that when our Love Bank is depleted, we're more likely to hurt our spouse than anyone else. What a tragedy!

The secret to avoiding this tragedy, of course, is to avoid losing love units once they've been deposited. All the best intentions, sin-cere vows, and honest efforts cannot substitute for a substantial Love Bank account. The Love Bank determines whom we marry and it usually determines whether or not we'll be divorced. Therefore it is tremendously important to understand how to sustain Love Bank accounts—how to avoid withdrawals once deposits have been made.

Falling Out of Love Is Not Inevitable

Romantic love feels spectacular! It inspires poets, musicians, artists, theologians, philosophers, and hosts of others to try to understand it, explain it, describe it, and experience it. It's just a feeling, but a feeling that people are willing to do extraordinary things to achieve.

Romantic love is also an incredible motivator—for both good and bad. It motivates married couples to take special care of each other but it has also motivated political, business, and religious leaders throughout history to throw away their influence, ethical values, fortunes, and health to leave their spouse to be with someone else they loved.

But in most marriages, and most affairs, romantic love doesn't last. And when a relationship loses romantic love, much of the instinctive motivation to show special care and consideration vanishes.

Imagine how difficult it would be for you to show affection, reveal personal thoughts and feelings, and make love to someone you don't love, someone you may even hate. Perhaps, as you are reading this book, you find yourself in that very position. It's an absolute nightmare for most people.

Romantic love inspires people to marry each other because it makes affection and intimacy seem natural and instinctive, but when romantic love fades and you're still expected to behave romantically, serious instinctive conflicts emerge. You simply don't feel romantic—and without that feeling, it's difficult, if not impossible, to meet the romantic needs of your spouse or have your spouse meet yours. You find yourself avoiding such intimate experiences.

To many, this process of falling *out of* love seems inevitable. Some "experts" have concluded that romantic love simply can't last throughout marriage. Some marriage counselors who feel that way encourage couples to divorce after love has gone. Others encourage couples to stick it out for the sake of the children, economics, religious values, and other considerations.

While it's true that divorce leads to disaster from every point of view, marriage without romantic love also leads to disaster—emotional disaster. I don't encourage couples to divorce but I also don't encourage them to endure marriage without romantic love. Instead, I encourage them to *restore* the romantic love they once had for each other.

How can you do this? In simple banking terms, you need to make more deposits and fewer withdrawals.

There were three chapters in the story of Jim and Karen's marriage before I counseled with them. In the first chapter they met each other's emotional needs, deposited love units, and were in love with each other. In the second chapter they stopped meeting some of these important emotional needs and their deposits were fewer and farther between. Their frustrations with unmet needs opened the third chapter. Instead of solving their problems thoughtfully, they chose to hurt each other. This selfish strategy poked gaping holes in their love bank accounts, and love units poured out.

In this book I will not try to teach you how to deposit love units by meeting each other's emotional needs. I have already done that in another book I wrote, *His Needs, Her Needs*. Instead, I will teach you how to avoid the tragic mistake that Jim and Karen made in response to their frustration. When they chose to hurt each other, they chose to withdraw love units from each other's Love Banks. That choice destroyed what love they had left for each other.

There's no point in trying to meet emotional needs when you are being thoughtless at the same time. It's like pouring water into a sieve. All the love units you deposit drain right out of the Love Bank. All your efforts to care are wasted. It's only when you know how to stop making withdrawals that your deposits make sense.

In the chapters that follow, you will learn how to avoid making Love Bank withdrawals. Once you learn these lessons, your efforts to meet each other's needs will reap huge dividends. The love units you deposit in each other's Love Bank will pile up, and you'll be in love with each other again.

What Are Love Busters?

Whenever you do something that makes your spouse unhappy, you withdraw love units. But let's face it, it's impossible to avoid all the bumps and bruises of life, especially *marital* bumps and bruises. Even in the best marriages, spouses hurt each other now and then.

Occasional mistakes do not drain a Love Bank, as long as they're seen as mistakes. An apology quickly heals the wound and the deposits continue unabated.

But when a mistake turns into a habit, repeated again and again, Love Bank accounts are at risk. In these situations, apologies mean very little because nothing is done to keep the love units from flowing out of the Love Bank. I call these habits that drain the Love Bank **Love Busters,** because they do more to ruin romantic love than anything else.

> A Love Buster is repeated behavior of one spouse that causes the other spouse to be unhappy (withdraws love units).

Through years of marriage counseling, I've been made aware of a host of Love Busters. Most of them fall into five categories: angry outbursts, disrespectful judgments, annoying behavior, selfish demands, and dishonesty. Because each of these categories is so important, I will discuss them one at a time in the following chapters and show you how to overcome them.

Then, in the second part of this book, I will show you how these Love Busters prevent couples from resolving common marital conflicts. You'll also see how easy it is to resolve these conflicts once the Love Busters are overcome.

In marriage you have an unprecedented opportunity to make your spouse happy. You do that whenever you meet his or her most important emotional needs. But you are also in a position to make your spouse miserable, more miserable than anyone else can. In all too many marriages, people choose to make each other miserable. When they come to me with their marital problems, my ultimate goal is to teach them how to make each other happy. But before I can get to that goal, I must first teach them how to stop hurting each other.

By the time you finish this book, you will know how to protect your spouse from yourself and your Love Busters. You'll be able to keep the love in your marriage from slipping away.

The Parable of the Net

Marriage is like a fishing net. Each day fishermen use their nets to catch fish and sell them at the market.

One fisherman takes his fish from the net every day but lets debris from the ocean accumulate. Eventually so much debris is caught in the net that he can hardly cast the net out of the boat, and when he does, it's almost impossible to retrieve. Finally, in a fit of anger, he cuts the net loose and goes home without it. He's unable to catch and sell fish again until he buys another net.

Another fisherman removes debris every time he retrieves the net with the fish he caught. Each time he casts his net, it's clean and ready to catch more fish. As a result, he catches and sells enough fish to support himself and his family.

In this parable, the fish are emotional needs met in marriage and the debris are Love Busters, habits that cause unhappiness.

Bad marriages are like the first fisherman's net. Angry outbursts, disrespectful judgments, annoying behavior, selfish demands, and dishonesty accumulate over time. The burden of the unhappiness they cause ruins a couple's willingness and ability to meet each other's emotional needs. Eventually the marriage supplies no benefits to either spouse and ends in divorce or emotional separation.

Good marriages are like the second fisherman's net. Love Busters are eliminated as soon as they appear, making it easy for the spouses to meet each other's emotional needs. Love grows because the Love Busters are tossed overboard.

Part 1

THE FIVE
LOVE BUSTERS

Angry Outbursts 2

Who Wants to Live with a Time Bomb?

Jill's father was kind and generous 99 percent of the time. But during that other 1 percent, he terrorized the entire household with his anger. So even though Jill's boyfriend, Sam, lost his temper once in a while, she considered him well-mannered compared to her father's outrageous behavior. Sam didn't hit anybody, he didn't break furniture, and he was never arrested for disorderly conduct—a real gentleman!

Before they married, Sam directed his anger away from Jill. He'd curse other drivers on the road, he'd fume over his boss's foolish decisions, and he'd become irate when salespeople failed to wait on him quickly. Jill did many of the same things, so she just chalked this up to human nature.

One morning soon after they were married, both Sam and Jill overslept and were running late. As they scurried about, getting dressed, Sam suddenly had a problem.

"Jill, I'm out of clean shirts," he shouted.

She didn't quite know how to respond. Since they both worked, Jill and Sam usually washed and ironed their own clothes. Once in a while, Jill would help Sam out but she had not agreed to take over the responsibility.

Jill tried to lighten up the situation. "I don't think any of mine will fit you," she joked.

"Was that supposed to be funny?" Sam shot back.

"Wear the one you wore yesterday," Jill suggested, trying to be helpful.

But Sam had already decided that, somehow, she was at fault. "You had to notice that I was out of shirts last night," he bellowed.

"Me, notice your shirts? Please, get serious." With that she turned to finish getting ready herself.

"I'm not done talking to you. You knew I was out of shirts, didn't you?"

"No," she said, "I didn't know you were out of shirts. But even if I did, it's your problem, not mine."

With that, Sam flew into a rage, complete with recriminations, condemnations, and obscenities.

Jill started to cry. This was the first time Sam had directed his anger toward her. Although he was not being violent, it hurt her deeply. Sam left the room, and nothing more was said about the incident.

This angry outburst was the first of many Jill would endure during the first year of their marriage. The pattern would always be the same: Sam would have a problem, blame Jill for it, and lose his temper; she would cry, and he would back off. As time passed, however, the frequency of these outbursts increased.

They were planning to have children, but Jill wisely chose to see a marriage counselor first. She was afraid Sam's anger would eventually turn into the mayhem she had witnessed as a child.

Jill was wise to see a marriage counselor for another reason. Sam's minor outbursts had punched a hole in her Love Bank—it had sprung a leak. After one year of marriage, she was losing the feeling of romantic love for Sam.

Every time Sam lost his temper, he was punishing Jill. This was a double hurt for Jill—she not only suffered from his punishing anger but also from the shocking realization that he was *trying* to hurt her. The man who had committed himself to her protection had become her greatest threat.

Why do couples destroy the love they have for each other with angry outbursts? In most cases, they don't understand the effect on love that anger has. Often one partner is trying to teach the other a lesson—the one partner feels hurt and angrily tries to show the other how that feels. And in most cases, the angry partner does not expect this punishment to ruin their love—after all, they promised to love each other forever.

They may have made the promise, but it was one they could not keep. People's feelings for each other are determined, not by promises, but by the Love Bank. When couples deliberately try to hurt each other, they deplete their Love Bank accounts. Romantic love becomes the victim of their anger.

Anger: A Threat to Your Spouse's Safety

Anger is the feeling that other people cause your unhappiness and they'll keep upsetting you until they're punished. They can't be reasoned with; the only thing they understand is pain and personal loss. Once you inflict that punishment, they'll think twice about making you unhappy again!

Anger's solution to a problem is to punish the troublemaker. This emotion overrides intelligence, which knows that punishment usually doesn't solve problems; it only makes the people you punish angry, which causes them to inflict punishment on you.

Anger also wins out over your commitment to provide safety and security for your spouse. When you become angry and try to hurt your spouse, your marriage is no longer safe. You are failing to protect your spouse from yourself.

Each of us has a private arsenal of weapons we can use when we're angry. If we think someone deserves to be punished, we're able to unlock the gate and select an appropriate weapon. Sometimes the weapons are verbal (ridicule and sarcasm), sometimes they're devious plots to cause suffering, and sometimes they're physical. But they have one thing in common: the ability to hurt people. And we can hurt our spouse more than anyone.

Most of the angry husbands and wives I've counseled have fairly harmless arsenals—like Sam's outbursts. Others are extremely dangerous. Many of my clients have been arrested for physical abuse and some have spent time in prison for beating their spouse. Most are remorseful at first but after they go through a time of hand-wringing, the conversation usually turns to lessons their spouse needs to learn. The bottom line for most of these clients is that they feel their spouse deserves the punishment.

When a relationship becomes violent—when angry outbursts reach extreme levels—there is a good chance that it's too risky for the abused partner to stick around and try to restore romantic love. Working with abusive clients, I have discovered that even successful therapy does not suddenly end their abusive acts but brings about only a gradual decrease. This would be fine when we're dealing with, say, name-calling—an occasional slipup during the therapeutic process will not threaten the safety of a spouse. But it's quite another matter when the occasional failure takes the form of attempted murder.

I've listened patiently to husbands who have sworn never to hit their wife again, but by the next time I see them, they've inflicted even more bruises and broken bones. One man claimed to be "cured" in a religious service of his violent tendencies, then tried to kill his wife a short time later. Another man attempted to kill his wife three times before she finally divorced him. I have witnessed many cases of murdered or permanently injured men and women who gave their spouse one chance too many.

Your anger is one of the greatest threats to your spouse's safety. Even if the weapons you use in an angry outburst are not life threatening or disabling, you can still inflict a great deal of fear. Without a doubt it's a Love Buster.

Overcoming Angry Outbursts

Sam was not so sure he had a problem with angry outbursts but that's a common perspective of those who can't seem to control their temper.

Anger is deceitful: It lets you forget what really happened and offers you a distortion of the truth. When Jill described one of Sam's angry outbursts to me, he shook his head in disbelief. "It just didn't happen that way," he said in all sincerity. "I don't understand why you would tell Dr. Harley such a thing."

Of course, I wasn't at the scene, but experience has taught me to give the benefit of the doubt to the victim. When couples have tape recorded their fights, the one having the outburst is usually amazed at what he or she said.

Anger is also cunning: It tries to convince your intelligence that anger is an appropriate reaction. Sam felt that Jill "made him" angry. If she had been more considerate, he would not have lost his temper. So it was her fault.

Many of my violent clients, both men and women, have told me that their spouses had it coming to them, that they deserved the angry reaction their thoughtless behavior aroused.

How do you go about stripping anger's deceit and cunning from outbursts so that anger can be seen for what it is? It's an ugly monster. How do you remove the screen that it hides behind?

Step 1: Identify instances of angry outbursts and their effects.

Sam had to begin with the facts. Did he have a problem with anger or didn't he? My first step in helping him overcome angry outbursts was to uncover the monster—describing Sam's angry reactions and their effects on Jill. The person in the best position to describe the problem was Jill.

So I had Jill answer the following questions:

1. On a scale from 0 to 6, with 0 indicating no unhappiness and 6 extreme unhappiness, what number most accurately reflects how much unhappiness you experience when your spouse attacks you with an angry outburst?
2. How often does your spouse tend to attack you with an angry outburst?
3. When your spouse attacks you with an angry outburst, what does he or she typically do? List the ways you are attacked.
4. Which of the ways you are attacked cause you the greatest unhappiness?
5. When did your spouse first attack you with an angry outburst?
6. Have your spouse's angry outbursts increased or decreased in intensity and/or frequency since they first began?
7. How do recent angry outbursts compare with those of the past?

I've counseled many who, after reading their spouse's answers to these questions, simply laugh. They are amazed that their spouse would write down what my clients think are lies about their behavior. The deceit and cunning of their anger blind them to the truth. In some cases, they even lose their tempers as they are reading the answers. That's why I never have their spouse present at this time. Sometimes I don't include the spouse in any of the sessions until I can get past this step. We cannot make any progress toward a solution until the perpetrator of violence sees anger for what it is: a threat to the safety and security of the spouse—and the marriage.

Jill's answers to these questions defined the problem and made it clear that Sam was making her unhappy with his angry outbursts. That was reason enough to do something about it. As Sam and I looked over Jill's answers, tears came to his eyes.

Sam saw that Jill had rated her unhappiness a 6, "extremely unhappy." He didn't want her to be unhappy and certainly didn't want to be the cause of her unhappiness.

What he had seen as an honest expression of his frustration, she interpreted as an ambush, a painful attack. His method of communicating his feelings had turned him into her worst enemy.

Sam's vicious attacks on Jill's character and judgment were hardest on her. He would tell her how selfish she was, how he was doing everything for her and she was doing nothing for him. He also would berate her abilities, charging that her only value was in her figure, not in her head.

His rantings simply weren't true. She did many things to prove her care for him and she was a highly skilled legal secretary, in great demand because of her knowledge and clerical ability. Sam's angry outbursts were filled with statements made to hurt her, not to solve his problem.

Jill described the shirt incident as the first time she felt attacked by his angry outbursts. She had been a witness to his anger prior to that incident but until then it had not been directed toward her. She went on to describe his recent attacks and how they had become more frequent and more abusive. Jill also said that she was unwilling to raise children in an environment overshadowed by the threat of violence.

After Sam finished reading Jill's answers to the questions, he agreed to stop losing his temper. He made no excuses and, for once, agreed with her interpretation of the problem. We were ready to go to the next step.

Step 2: Understand why angry outbursts take place.

Now it was Sam's turn to answer a few questions. Why did he do it? Why did he lose his temper? I gave him the following questions to answer before our next appointment.

1. What are the most important reasons that you use angry outbursts to punish your spouse?

2. When you use angry outbursts to punish your spouse, what do you typically do?
3. When you use angry outbursts to punish your spouse, what hurts your spouse the most?
4. After you use angry outbursts to punish your spouse, do you usually feel better about the situation than before you used them? Why or why not?
5. Do you feel that punishment evens the score and that without it your spouse wins and you lose? Explain.
6. Do you ever try to control or avoid using angry outbursts to punish your spouse? If so, why do you do it? How do you do it?
7. If you were to decide never to use angry outbursts to punish your spouse again, would you be able to stop? Why or why not?
8. Are you willing to stop using angry outbursts to punish your spouse? Why or why not?

There is something about all of these questions that should jump out at you. Do you see it? Each question assumes that angry outbursts are *intended* to be a punishment. As it turns out, one of the ways people deceive themselves about anger is to interpret it as something other than punishment. One of my clients called it an expression of his creativity. Another viewed anger as a cry for help. I probably haven't heard them all but I've heard hundreds of ways that perpetrators of violence have downplayed what anger really is. It's punishment, pure and simple.

The purpose of angry outbursts is to inflict pain and suffering on the target. Any other interpretation is part of anger's deception. When the deception is removed and you see it for what it is—punishment—it's much easier to ask the question *why?*

Sam understood that he was punishing Jill whenever she was the target of his anger. As he answered the questions in the privacy of his home, he began to uncover the reasons. After they were married, he had a growing feeling that he was no longer important to her. His feelings were hurt whenever she made her work a higher priority than his interests. So whenever he lost his temper, he attacked her career, which he felt was coming between them. But he also attacked Jill.

As we went through his answers, he realized that he was using anger to even the score, to make her feel some of the pain he felt. He admitted that after an outburst he felt a little better. At least he had expressed his frustration instead of keeping it bottled inside of him.

Sam didn't think it would take much effort to control his temper. He would just have to make the decision to stop and that would be that. Most people with angry outbursts feel that way. Some are right, but time would tell if he was being realistic.

When Sam made a commitment to Jill that she would never again be the target of his anger, he thought that was the end of the issue. He had seen the error of his ways and he had decided to change. They wouldn't need to see a counselor anymore, right? Wrong! Poor Sam, he had only completed the second step. There were three more to go.

Step 3: Try to avoid the conditions that tend to trigger angry outbursts.

Before Sam left my office, I gave him a few more questions to answer for our next session. They concerned the angry outbursts we had been discussing in the assignment he had just completed:

1. In the instances of angry outbursts that you identified earlier, describe the conditions that seemed to trigger them. Include your physical condition (amount of sleep, physical health, etc.), setting, people present, behavior of those people, your mental state, and any other relevant information.
2. What changes in any of those conditions or efforts to avoid those conditions might help you stop angry outbursts in the future?
3. What changes identified in question 2 can be made with your spouse's enthusiastic agreement?
4. Describe your plan, which can be made with your spouse's enthusiastic agreement to change or avoid the conditions. In-

clude a deadline that also meets with his or her enthusiastic agreement.

When a husband and wife come to an agreement, I want it to be an *enthusiastic* one. Halfhearted, self-sacrificing arrangements generally fall apart the first time they're tested. So any changes that would help Sam control his temper had to be agreed to enthusiastically by Jill.

Sam felt that mornings were worst for him and that he tended to wake up irritable. Little things that Jill would do or say bothered him terribly at that time of the day. Later in the day, he seemed to have a completely different outlook on life and he could handle irritations much better.

Jill's job was Sam's greatest source of frustration. Whenever she talked about it, particularly when she talked about her boss, it drove him nuts. He saw her job in general and her boss in particular as great threats to their future. Sam expected that Jill would eventually have an affair with her boss.

It is quite common for jealous husbands or wives to be angry with their spouse. The threat of something or someone coming between them makes them furious. Their anger, of course, doesn't begin to solve the problem. In fact it tends to drive their spouse into the arms of anyone who will save him or her from the terror experienced in marriage. Whether or not Sam had anything to fear from Jill's boss, his anger greatly increased the risk of an affair.

Angry outbursts are an inappropriate way to approach a marital conflict. It makes the solution much more difficult. The conflict that Sam had with Jill over her work and her relationship with her boss could be resolved, but not with the threat of an angry outburst.

So I encouraged Sam to resolve his conflict with Jill *after* he had learned to control his temper, rather than making it a *condition* to control his temper. It's like negotiating with terrorists. Whatever they demand, you cannot let them have it. They must remove the threat to innocent citizens before you discuss a resolution. Otherwise they will use that threat every time they want something.

Sam's early-morning irritability was another matter entirely. Jill was perfectly willing to avoid discussing conflicts with him in the morning, and Sam also agreed. So they decided that their morning conversation would be limited to "please pass the milk," avoiding any unpleasant topics.

Step 4: When you cannot avoid conditions that trigger angry outbursts, find an individual or support group to hold you accountable.

Before the session was over, we discussed the fact that Sam had made a commitment to control his temper regardless of the conditions. In other words, even though Jill seemed to put her career interests before Sam's interests, he was not to express his frustration with an angry outburst.

From the perspective of an angry spouse, the solution is simple: *Stop doing what irritates me and I'll control my temper.* But any anger management therapist knows that a plan like that gets a person nowhere. The truth is, there are many situations in life, especially in marriage, where we cannot make others do what we want them to. People will do irritating things, there's no getting around it.

The goal of anger management is to avoid an angry outburst when you're irritated the most, when people seem the most insensitive. To achieve that objective, it's a good idea to find a person or group to hold you accountable. For Sam, I was that person.

Although Sam thought he would have no trouble controlling his temper, just to be on the safe side he agreed to call me three times a week. I still met him for weekly appointments, but his five-minute calls were for support and accountability.

Step 5: Measure your progress.

Before Sam left my office, I invited Jill to join us and handed her a form with these instructions:

Please list all instances of your spouse's angry outbursts and acts that you consider punishment for something you did. These include

*verbal and physical acts of anger and threatened acts of anger toward
you, cursing you, and making disrespectful or belittling comments
about you. Include the day, date, time, and circumstances, along with
a description of each angry outburst.*

I asked Jill to keep a record of how well Sam kept his commitment
to control his temper. Measuring progress is the most critical step in
this plan to overcome angry outbursts, and the victim is usually the
best one to do the measuring. Jill, more than anyone else, would
know when Sam slipped up. As I mentioned earlier, anger tries to
make us forget what it did, so those who have difficulty controlling
their anger are not good at measuring their own progress. Furthermore, Jill's documentation would be a big help in understanding pre-
cisely what it was that bothered her so much.

Before they left my office, I told Sam that he would have to accept
as truth whatever Jill wrote down. He was not to argue with her about
her interpretation of his behavior, but just try to avoid doing it in the
future. I warned him that there would be some surprises the first week.

Sure enough, when he called me the first time for his five-minute
session, she had already written down two instances of angry outbursts—and one of them was in the parking lot on the way out of
my office.

"Why is she doing this to me?" Sam complained. "I didn't lose
my temper. All I did was tell her that we didn't need to go through
all of this. Can't I express my feelings anymore?"

I hadn't seen Jill's report, so I didn't know what he had said. But
I explained that this was one of the surprises I had warned Sam about.
It was important for him to understand exactly how Jill interpreted
his "expression of feelings." To her it was punishment. I suggested
that to be on the safe side, he should not express his frustration to
her but to me instead.

Two days later, I talked to him again on the telephone, and he
proudly announced that Jill had made no new entries since my last
conversation with him. For the very first time he realized that his
expression of frustration with Jill threatened her and made her

unhappy. He would need to learn how to talk to her in a way that would make her feel safe.

When I saw Jill and Sam for their next appointment, I talked with Jill first and read the entries in her progress report. She explained how difficult it had been to be truthful, because she was afraid that the report itself would cause Sam to lose his temper. It's true. Some of my clients have reacted to the report with angry outbursts. One man actually tore it up when he read it because he did not agree with his wife's analysis.

Whenever that happens, it brings into focus the seriousness of the client's problem. In some cases a more intense plan of action must be created to address the fact that the anger is out of control. Sometimes I encourage couples to separate until a client can prove enough control to guarantee the spouse's safety.

Sam was able to stop being verbally abusive and he was able to reduce his feeling of anger toward Jill. He explained to me how he did it.

"I know what makes me feel angry. It is thinking that Jill doesn't really care about me and all she cares about is herself. But if I can relax and tell myself she really does care and that we will be able to work out our problems eventually, I don't feel as angry."

Jill really did care about Sam and wanted to have a family with him someday. She was definitely on his side and wanted him to succeed in controlling his anger. Within a few weeks, they were engaged in serious negotiations about the way her work affected him, and she made some very important changes to accommodate his feelings. His anger had driven her away from him, and now that he proved he could protect her from it, she was drawn closer to him, something he had wanted all along.

They also came to some very important agreements regarding child-rearing techniques. I warned them that Sam's anger could easily be directed toward their children, and that would also withdraw love units from Jill's Love Bank. So they both agreed that any discipline would be mutually agreed to, *enthusiastically* agreed to, or it wouldn't happen.

People with a predisposition to anger are also predisposed to bad marriages and, ultimately, divorce. But if you can recognize anger for what it really is, a monster, and learn how to protect your spouse from it, you not only save your marriage, but you also save yourself from a life of endless searching for someone you can get along with.

Despite what some people think, controlling your anger does not lead to serious emotional problems. I've counseled hundreds of people who have been successful in protecting their spouse from their angry outbursts, and none of them went crazy. Instead, they felt a lot better about themselves, and their spouses felt downright emancipated.

As I've said over and over, anger has no place in marriage. While it is a normal human reaction, it is also a destructive reaction, and you must protect your spouse from it if your spouse is to be happy and secure living with you.

Disrespectful Judgments 3

Who Wants to Live with a Critic?

inda was raised by parents who worked long hours but never seemed to get ahead. The major reason for their low income was their lack of education—neither parent graduated from high school. But their large family—five children—was also a contributing factor. Linda, her three brothers, one sister, and their parents shared a small house and just about everything else throughout her childhood.

After graduating from high school, Linda found a job as a receptionist, which paid enough to support her. So at eighteen, she moved away from home, rented an apartment, bought her own car, and felt on top of the world.

Tom, a new executive, found Linda very attractive. At first, he just greeted her whenever he passed her desk, but the greetings turned into conversations and before long he was regularly having lunch with her. Eventually he fell in love.

Tom was well educated, having earned advanced degrees in both law and business administration. When he met Linda's family, he was immediately accepted and respected by them all. Her father was especially pleased that she chose to date such an intelligent man.

At first, Tom had respect for Linda and her family as well. But as their romance developed, he began making critical remarks about the decisions made by members of her family. Then, occasionally, he began to criticize Linda's decisions. Since he was so well educated, she assumed in most instances that he was correct and she was wrong. It bothered her whenever he made these critical remarks but it happened so seldom that it had little negative effect on her growing love for him.

Before long they were married, and after the honeymoon Tom and Linda returned to work as husband and wife. But their relationship at work changed the very first day: Linda found herself working with her worst critic, who also happened to be her husband.

Now that they were married, Tom became more critical than he was before. He would bring the smallest errors to her attention and coach her on improving her posture, telephone etiquette, and other office skills.

Of course, she became increasingly unhappy at work and eventually decided to quit so she could prepare for having children. Her income, after taxes, was not enough to make much of a difference in their standard of living anyway, and Tom earned enough to support them both. Besides, she was raised to value the role of a homemaker and full-time mother.

But as soon as she quit her job, she went from the frying pan into the fire. At home Tom became even more critical than he'd been at work. He expected her to develop a high level of homemaking skills and critically evaluated her work each day. Her performance rarely met his standards, so she just gave up. Before long, she was spending the day watching television and sleeping.

Since his lectures on homemaking didn't seem to help, Tom turned his attention to subjects of motivation and ambition. When he came home from work, Linda had to suffer through Tom's self-improvement courses. Their discussions became so one-sided that she eventually stopped trying to explain her point of view.

Tom thought he was doing her a favor. He was not angry when he criticized her and was not trying to punish her. He was genuinely concerned about her and felt that his criticism was helping her. But he was making a far greater mistake than all of her mistakes combined: He was failing to protect her from the pain she felt whenever he made a critical comment. His "help" was causing her to become very depressed and his lectures withdrew all the love units from her Love Bank. Before long Linda had lost her feeling of love for Tom.

Linda became so depressed that Tom decided that she needed professional help. He made an appointment to speak with me alone, to determine my competence. After I passed his test, he brought her with him to the second session and wanted to be included in the interview. But I asked to speak with Linda alone, and he remained in the waiting room. Within two sessions, however, I had Tom join her—for marriage counseling.

You're Always Right?

Have you ever tried to straighten out your spouse? Occasionally we're all tempted to do that sort of thing. At the time, we think we're doing our spouse a big favor, to lift him or her from the darkness of confusion into the light of our "superior perspectives." We think that if our spouse would only follow our advice, he or she could avoid many of life's pitfalls.

Yet, if we're not careful, our effort to keep our spouse from making mistakes can lead to a much bigger mistake, one that destroys romantic love. The mistake is called *disrespectful judgments*.

A disrespectful judgment occurs whenever someone tries to *impose* his or her system of values and beliefs on someone else. If you ever try to force your spouse to accept your point of view, you're just asking for trouble.

Most of us feel that our judgment is correct. When we hear others express opposing views, we sometimes feel that their opinions will get them into trouble someday. If it's your spouse disagreeing with you, naturally you want to save him or her from the pain that this mistake will create. So you try to change your spouse's opinion.

The trouble starts when you assume you have the right, and sometimes the responsibility, to *impose* your opinions on your spouse. Almost invariably, this imposition will be regarded as personally threatening, arrogant, rude, and incredibly disrespectful. That's when you lose love units.

It's disrespectful to try to impose your opinions on your spouse because when you do, you imply that he or she has poor judgment. If you valued your spouse's judgment, you would question your own opinions. It could be that your spouse is right and you are wrong. At the very least, you would try to understand his or her position more fully.

If you respect your spouse's judgment, you will discuss any conflicting issue with a willingness to change your mind. In the process, the two of you learn something from each other. That's how *respectful persuasion* works.

In marriage the blending of a husband and wife's value systems brings benefit to both. Each partner brings wisdom and foolishness to the marriage. By respectfully discussing beliefs and values, the couple has an opportunity to create a superior system. But the task must be approached with mutual respect if it is to work. Without that respect, the husband and wife cannot improve their values and they will lose romantic love for each other.

Ridicule Doesn't Work

When Linda became seriously depressed, Tom assumed that she had not learned the lessons he tried to teach her, so he pressed them with even greater diligence. But the harder he pressed, the more depressed she became. He was so convinced he was right that it never occurred to him that his disrespectful judgments were causing her depression.

The first time I spoke with Linda, she explained how unpleasant her life had become since she married Tom. She never liked housework in the first place, and now Tom expected her to become a professional home economist. A whole lifetime of housework loomed before her. Raising children no longer appealed to her, because it would only increase the housework she had come to hate. She felt useless and trapped. If that wasn't bad enough, her sexual attraction to Tom had disappeared entirely. Everything he expected of her had become impossible to perform.

In my session with Tom, I laid out my perspective of the problem as respectfully as I could. I didn't want to make the same mistake he'd made by imposing my view on him. I wanted my counseling to be an example of respectful persuasion.

I explained to him that, in his effort to help his wife, he'd apparently overlooked her emotional reactions. Perhaps his advice would have helped if Linda's feelings had been taken into account. But because he overlooked her feelings, his advice had been misinterpreted. Her depression was, in part, caused by his flawed approach to helping her.

Since Tom cared a great deal for Linda and wanted her to be healthy and happy, he was willing to test my theory for a few months. If she recovered from her depression, he was willing to make the changes permanent.

I focused attention on the way Tom and Linda made decisions. Until they came to my office, Tom tried to make many of Linda's decisions for her. And he rarely consulted her about her feelings on those issues. Linda had very little confidence in her own judgment, and the longer she'd been married, the more convinced she became that Tom was smarter—so he should make all the decisions.

But that wasn't her only problem. Whenever Linda expressed an opinion, Tom tended to ridicule her. He often thought her ideas were stupid and told her so whenever she expressed herself. He was incredibly disrespectful.

The Policy of Joint Agreement

If Tom was to overcome his disrespectful judgments, he needed to make Linda an equal partner in their decision making. He needed to respect her perspective on each issue they faced. So I ventured forth with a plan to teach Tom how to make decisions that would respect Linda's opinions.

Before training them in respectful decision making, I gave Tom and Linda a new rule to follow. I call the rule the **Policy of Joint Agreement:** Never do anything without an enthusiastic agreement between you and your spouse.

This rule gave Tom a whole new perspective on negotiating with Linda. From then on, he could never force his way of thinking on her, because that approach would not result in her enthusiastic agreement. He could not shame her; he could not talk over her; he could not ridicule her. None of those would work. He had to *persuade* her. And he had to be so persuasive that she would enthusiastically agree with him.

Up to the day Tom was introduced to the Policy of Joint Agreement, he rarely discussed his plans with Linda and didn't feel he needed her approval. He believed he was being thoughtful when he merely told her what he was doing, and when he bothered to get Linda's reluctant agreement to his plans, he was going the extra mile!

But from that day forward, everything Tom did had to meet with Linda's *enthusiastic* agreement. I knew he'd find the rule incredibly difficult to follow at first and I expected him to make many mistakes. But it would set him on a course that would eventually lead Linda out of her depression and ultimately save their marriage.

The Policy of Joint Agreement

Never do anything without an enthusiastic agreement between you and your spouse.

After Tom and Linda agreed to follow the Policy of Joint Agreement, we focused attention on their joint decision making. To get an enthusiastic agreement with Linda, Tom had to learn to treat her perspective and feelings with respect. At the same time, Linda needed help in developing a higher regard for her own perspective and feelings.

Can a Spouse Ever Be Critical?

Some disrespectful judgments don't directly reflect on the character or value of your spouse. For example, if you try to impose your political perspective on your spouse, your focus is on politics, not on your spouse. But your spouse is sure to be offended because you make the assumption that your judgment regarding the issue is sound and your spouse's judgment is flawed. You will surely withdraw love units.

But when disrespectful judgments *do* reflect on the character or value of your spouse, you're really in trouble. Not only are you devaluing your spouse's judgment, but you're also devaluing your spouse. Those disrespectful judgments are the worst kind. They're called *criticism*.

Think with me for a minute. Can you ever be critical of your spouse without being disrespectful? Well, it depends on what you mean by "criticism." When we use the word, we usually mean that we're judging something unfavorably—after we've seen it, we don't like it.

While it's true that we use the words "critical acclaim" to reflect a favorable judgment, that's not what we usually mean when we say we're critical. When we're critical, we are usually judging unfavorably.

My wife, Joyce, is a professional vocalist and recording artist. As her career was developing, I wanted to help her in every way I could. One way I thought I could help was to make suggestions to perfect her performances.

Joyce encouraged me to be critical because she wanted to improve. Most of my comments were genuinely supportive, since she's quite talented. But whenever I gave her a critical "helpful suggestion," she became visibly upset. I withdrew love units each time.

To this day she wants me to honestly evaluate her performances, yet whenever I find fault, my account in her Love Bank suffers. Granted, I don't lose as many love units as I would if I tried to force my standards on her, insisting that she sing the way I want her to. That would be blatantly disrespectful. But any negative comments I make take something away from our relationship. So even *respectful* criticism is usually interpreted as being disrespectful. After all, the criticism itself is a form of disrespect.

I've come to the conclusion that lovers should not be each other's critics. There are countless examples of people we've seen on television and in the movies who married their managers. These marriages, by and large, suffer greatly because the manager keeps on managing after the marriage, destroying the feelings of love in the process.

I hasten to add that I've always been honest with Joyce when she asks for my opinion. I do not give her a false impression just to make her feel good. But it's one thing to sit back and enjoy one of her concerts as a fan, and quite another to view it through the eyes of a music critic. I'm definitely her fan.

At this point I can hear you asking, *But what can you do when you know your spouse is making a mistake? Do you just sit back and let the one you love fail?*

The answer is found in *respectful persuasion*. I'll use an illustration with which most of us can agree: the use of seat belts.

Let's say that your spouse is not in the habit of wearing a seat belt and you consider it important. So whenever you drive anywhere with your spouse, you offer a simple reminder to buckle up. Amazingly enough, your spouse may resent this. It may seem as if you are imposing your values on your spouse.

Now you might think that, with enough reminders, it will eventually become a habit, and your spouse won't need any more reminders. But that's not the way habits are formed—unless you're there to insure compliance *every time* your spouse enters a car.

So, no matter how good your intentions are, your constant harping on the seat belt issue will probably only irritate your spouse and not cause any lasting change in behavior. It's better to use respectful persuasion and let your spouse make his or her own decision on the matter.

With respectful persuasion, you would try to find a way to encourage seat belt use by taking your spouse's feelings into account. If I want Joyce to wear a seat belt, I need to understand why she does not wear one in the first place. The seat belt may make her feel confined, and forcing her to wear it would not only be disrespectful, it would also subject her to discomfort. I can present the case for protection in the event of a crash but I must let her choose between safety and comfort. That's respectful persuasion.

Even if you're convinced your spouse is seriously mistaken, any disrespectful judgments you make will backfire. Whenever you try to impose your way of thinking, you make your spouse feel bad—and you withdraw love units from the Love Bank. You may have the best of intentions, your spouse's happiness and fulfillment as the hoped-for outcome of your effort. But it won't work.

In marriage the way you go about doing things is usually more important than the things themselves. A far more effective approach to the problem is to try to understand the emotional basis for your spouse's habits and opinions and respectfully negotiate a change that takes those emotional reactions into account. At the same time, you should examine your own emotional reactions to understand what makes your habits and opinions comfortable to you. You'll not only find yourself resolving your conflicts with greater ease, but you will also protect the romantic love you have for each other.

Turning Disrespectful Judgments into Respectful Persuasion

Put yourself on the receiving end of disrespectful judgments. Few conversations are more irritating than those in which someone tries to force his opinion on you, and so you're seldom swayed by those who badger you. You end up wondering, *Why should I consider the point of view of someone who's so insensitive?* You don't *want* to be persuaded by someone who doesn't consider your perspective.

On the other hand, when someone makes an effort to consider your opinion before presenting his or her own, you're far more open to an alternative view.

One of a salesperson's first lessons is to understand the need of the prospective buyer before presenting a product. The prospective buyer will consider the product if it meets a need, *but if he or she doesn't need it,* the salesperson wastes everybody's time.

How often have you been called on the telephone (in the evening) by a telemarketing salesperson who wants to sell you a new telephone service? "I'm satisfied with my existing service," you answer, trying to explain that you have no need. But instead of politely ending the conversation, the telemarketer begins to read the sales pitch as if you had not spoken. I react to such an approach by mentally labeling that company as one I will never do business with, even if they offer me *free* telephone service!

Linda had such a low opinion of her judgment that I had to encourage her to become more assertive in expressing herself to Tom. Tom also had to learn to listen.

One of the most valuable lessons I taught Linda was to explain her opinions in emotional as well as logical terms. In other words, she could defend her position by simply explaining that it made her feel comfortable to think the way she did.

In the first few weeks that I counseled Linda and Tom, she began to express her opinions more openly and freely spoke in terms of her *feelings.* This was an eye-opener for Linda. Tom had been in the habit of justifying his decisions with his values and logic. If she told him his decision did not "feel" right to her, he would attack her values and argue that values were more important than feelings. Previously she had bought into his arguments, and when his decisions made her unhappy, she had concluded that something was wrong with her.

But now Linda realized that Tom's values were often nothing more than rationalizations of *his* feelings. For example, she noticed that if his feelings about something changed, his values would often change to accommodate them. Tom's feelings turned out to be more important than he had led her to believe.

I'm not suggesting that values simply serve our emotional predispositions. I am a firm believer in universal values that are true, regardless of how we feel about them. But when people use their values to force us to do something for them, watch out! People often couch their feelings in value statements. They have learned to get their way by appealing to "truth," when, in fact, their feelings lie behind their opinions all along.

If you wish to persuade your spouse to your way of thinking, you must first determine why your point of view would be an improvement. If your perspective would make life easier or more successful, then your appeal should be seriously considered. But if it makes *your* life easier *at your spouse's expense* (which is often the case), your selfish motives will make your position very weak.

In most cases, we want our spouse to change perspective for selfish reasons. You want something you haven't been getting. Your spouse is somewhat willing to do things for you just because he or she cares for you. But if you follow the Policy of Joint Agreement, wanting only what your spouse can do with enthusiasm, there must be something in it for him or her too.

If it's simply not in your spouse's best interest, just drop the subject and move on. But if you're certain that your perspective would be of value to your spouse, you need to introduce evidence to prove it. People are usually willing to try something for a while, and that may give you the chance to test the value of your perspective (but the test must not take much time or effort).

To explain this method, let me introduce five steps to respectful persuasion.

Step 1: Clearly state your conflicting opinions to each other.

When you have a disagreement, can you clearly explain *your spouse's* opinion? Many needless arguments arise because spouses misunderstand each other. Once you have stated your spouse's opinion (to your spouse's satisfaction), you may find you're not in disagreement after all.

Being able to state *your own* position clearly is another crucial step that will help your spouse understand your motives and true objectives. For example, if I want my wife to wear her seat belt, I might tell her that I care about her safety and it makes me nervous when she drives without her belt buckled up. This type of explanation helps her understand the emotional reasons behind my opinion.

In response to my concern for her welfare, she may explain to me that she doesn't wear a seat belt because it makes her feel confined and wrinkles her clothes. Explaining her position in emotional terms takes the issue away from the philosophical debate. It turns out that she is not opposed to people wearing seat belts. In fact she believes it is a good idea to wear them. She just doesn't feel it's necessary for *her.*

In this example, we are not in disagreement over the principle itself. We merely disagree over the application of the principle to my wife's behavior.

In fact most arguments are like this—not rooted in different beliefs but in differing *emotional reactions* to the application of beliefs. If Joyce *feels* bad when she wears seat belts, she will tend not to wear them.

If I tell her to wear seat belts, and wearing them makes her feel uncomfortable, I am causing her to lose love units for me in two different ways: First, people usually don't like to be told what to do; second, wearing seat belts makes her feel uncomfortable, and I'll be associated with that unpleasant feeling.

If I want to avoid losing love units, *she* must believe that my opinion is in her best interest. I try to achieve that objective in the second step.

Step 2: Explain how your opinion is in your spouse's best interest.

Why do husbands and wives have so much trouble discussing their differences? Because the process can be so unpleasant. Rather than discovering each other's emotional needs and working together toward mutual need satisfaction, they tend to ridicule each other. How long can a disrespectful conversation last before it becomes abusive?

Begin the process of explaining your opinion by showing respect for the opinion of your spouse. You might say, "Even though I don't agree with you, I know you have good reasons for your opinion. But I would like to suggest some other reasons that may change your mind."

Some people have great difficulty making the above statement because they don't believe their spouse has any good reasons for his or her opinions. This attitude reveals underlying disrespect. As the spouse tries to explain his or her reasons, each reason becomes the subject of ridicule, until the spouse finally learns not to voice his or her opinions.

Using our seat belt example, I would *not* want to shout at Joyce, "Can't you see how stupid you are when you don't wear your seat belt?" That would be ineffective and antagonizing. Instead, I might explain how unpleasant her life could become if she were thrown through the windshield. I might also point out her risk of being fined if the police stop her. On a more positive note, I could suggest that, once she adjusts to a seat belt, she will have greater control over her car and may feel more secure in her seat.

Respectful persuasion never involves an attack on your spouse's defenses. Joyce may disagree with me, saying that some people have been killed because they use seat belts—sometimes they are unable to unlock the strap to escape a burning automobile. I should accept the reasonableness of her defense. Remember, her initial problem was that seat belts made her feel confined. It's reasonable for her to fear being locked in a burning automobile, unable to escape.

Thus far in our discussion, I have tried to explain how my position is in Joyce's best interest, and she has explained that she doesn't agree with me. If I were to attack her explanation, it would probably get me nowhere. Instead, it's more prudent to take another approach: Simply ask her to test my opinion for a brief period of time to see if she likes it. This is the third step of respectful persuasion.

Step 3: Suggest a test of your opinion.
A final argument in defense of your position is "Try it. You'll like it!"

People often make a big mistake in marital "discussions" when they try to force each other to make a committed change rather than a temporary one. Joyce is not convinced that my opinion is correct for her, so expecting her to make a commitment to my position is ridiculous! But her curiosity about my opinion and her respect for me may encourage her to risk a test of my opinion.

I might suggest to Joyce that she try to wear her seat belt each day for a week and see how she feels about it at the end of the week. In advance of the test, I would explain that habits take time to develop, so if she is comfortable with the first week's test, she may need to extend the test for about three months so that she will develop a habit of seat belt wearing.

In some situations, a test is not possible. For example, investing all your retirement savings into a new business pretty well commits you to the program, once you make the decision. But most examples of disrespectful judgments that I have encountered as a marriage counselor could have been reformulated to accommodate a test.

Step 4: If the test fails to persuade, drop the subject.

Clearly understand the bargain: If your spouse is not comfortable with your position after the test, you may ask for yet another test. But if your spouse feels the first test was sufficient, you must agree to drop the subject. At this point in respectful persuasion many couples forget the rules. The focus of attention should be on *respectful,* not on *persuasion.* If your test is ineffective in persuading your spouse, drop it. You may have another opportunity someday. But at this point you should back off.

If on the other hand your test is successful, resist the temptation to force a commitment to your position. If your spouse finds that your opinion works, it will automatically be incorporated into his or her judgment.

If Joyce were to try wearing her seat belt each day for a week and by the end of the week she were to find the experience reasonably comfortable, she would probably be willing to extend the test for three months, as we had originally agreed. The problem would probably take care of itself without further intervention on my part.

But if Joyce did not find that my test worked for her, I would be in no position to insist on another test or, worse yet, try to force my position on her. I may discuss the outcome of the test with her, trying to understand what went wrong and I can ask if she would be willing to try another one. But if she refuses, I should thank her for her willingness to try my first test and leave the subject alone.

Remember, respectful persuasion does nothing that would draw love units from your spouse's Love Bank. As soon as you do anything that your spouse finds unpleasant, it's no longer respectful persuasion. The entire process must be pleasant and nonthreatening. If you feel you must persuade your spouse at all costs, the cost will be love units, and you will probably fail to persuade. I may be able to force my wife to say she agrees with me and I may be able to force her to do what I want but I cannot force her to love me. Only the process of respectful persuasion can protect my account in her Love Bank.

Step 5: Give your spouse an opportunity to persuade you.

Respectful persuasion is a two-way street. My spouse has the right to try to influence my judgment just as much as I have the right to try to influence hers. Technically she has every right to try to convince me that wearing seat belts is a *bad* idea. Since most of us are convinced we should make a habit of wearing them, it's not a very reasonable illustration. Still, none of us has a corner on truth and we all can improve our judgments. Being open to the possibility that our loved one may be right about anything is a critical step toward respectful persuasion.

If I want to persuade my wife, I must be willing to let her persuade me. I must be open to the possibility that she could be right and I could be wrong about any issue we discuss.

Disrespectful Judge or Respectful Persuader?

How can you know if you're a perpetrator of disrespectful judgments? Ask your spouse. You may not realize how you come across.

But you are disrespectful if your spouse thinks you're disrespectful. That's the deciding factor.

I've made up the following questionnaire to help identify this particular Love Buster. Ask your spouse to answer these questions honestly. If your spouse identifies you as one who makes disrespectful judgments, you'll probably be tempted to make yet another disrespectful judgment and claim that he or she is wrong! Believe me, in this situation your spouse is the best judge by a long shot.

If you feel terribly uncomfortable having your spouse complete the questionnaire, or if your spouse would prefer not to, then do your best to answer the questions *as you think your spouse would.*

Disrespectful Judgments Questionnaire

Answer each question with a number from 1 to 7, 1 meaning "almost never," 4 meaning "sometimes," and 7 meaning "most of the time." Your answer should reflect your feelings about the way your spouse tries to influence your attitudes, beliefs, and behavior.

1. Does your spouse ever try to "straighten you out"?
2. Does your spouse ever lecture you instead of respectfully discussing issues?
3. Does your spouse seem to feel that his or her opinion is superior to yours?
4. When you and your spouse discuss an issue, does he or she interrupt you or talk so much it prevents you from having a chance to explain your position?
5. Are you afraid to discuss your point of view with your spouse?
6. Does your spouse ever ridicule your point of view?

The scoring of this questionnaire is simple. Unless all your spouse's answers are 1, you're probably engaging in disrespectful judgments. Almost all of us are guilty of this from time to time, so don't be alarmed if you get some 2s or 3s. But if your spouse gave you any 4s, 5s, 6s, or 7s, you're probably at risk of losing some of the romantic love in your marriage.

Don't make the mistake of winning the battle only to lose the war. An important part of romantic relationships is the support and encouragement lovers show each other. Disrespectful judgments do the opposite. If they have crept into your marriage, make an effort today to eliminate their destructive influence.

Imposing your point of view is bad enough. But when your point of view criticizes your spouse's character or value, you're making the biggest disrespectful judgment of all. If you ever hope to be in a romantic relationship with your spouse again, you must avoid critical generalizations at all costs.

Annoying Behavior 4

Who Wants to Live with a Dripping Faucet?

ong before she married Mike, Sharon knew that some of his habits irritated her. For instance, she didn't like the way he sat in a chair. She admired men who sat straight and tall, giving the impression that they were alert and attentive. When a man slouched in his chair, it reminded her of certain fat and lazy relatives.

But slouching was Mike's specialty—especially when he came home after work and parked in front of the TV.

"Mike, it really bothers me when you sit like that," she told him when they were newlyweds. "Please sit up in the chair."

Mike straightened up and continued watching television with a better posture, but a few minutes later he slumped back into the same position.

When Sharon returned to the room, she was always very disappointed. "Why do you sit like that, when you know it bothers me?"

Mike would quickly straighten up and say, "Oh, I'm sorry."

"You can't possibly be sorry. You just don't care how I feel."

"Look, Sharon," he'd answer, getting a little irritated. "I've had a hard day at work. Just don't look at me, and you'll feel much better."

Sharon would leave the room in tears, but Mike would be too absorbed in TV to notice. The first few times this happened, Sharon seethed with anger but after a while she began to doubt herself.

It's such a small thing, she thought. *He needs to relax after work, and I'm just being selfish to expect him to sit in his chair a certain way.*

So she decided to keep her feelings to herself. Whenever she saw Mike slumped in his chair, it still annoyed her but she didn't say anything. While the marriage seemed peaceful, Mike was losing love units with each slouch.

He never knew what was happening to his Love Bank account, and Sharon may not have been fully aware of it either. She didn't want to nag him about it because she felt he had a right to sit any way he chose, but still it bothered her. As time went on, Mike developed other annoying habits, but as with his sitting posture, Sharon felt she had no right to change him.

When they came to see me for counseling, Mike's poor posture had become only one example of many habits that made him an almost constant irritant to Sharon. She could hardly tolerate being with him for more than a few minutes at a time. Though she didn't believe in divorce, Sharon wanted a separation—she just couldn't imagine putting up with him for years to come.

Yet Mike's "bad" habits were all essentially innocent. They all fell into the same category as his sitting posture: eating habits, his tone of voice when he disciplined the children, phrases he overused, and his choice of clothes. None of these habits was "evil" or intentionally destructive, and Sharon knew this. Another woman might be delighted to have him for a husband, but his behavior drove Sharon up a wall. Though she felt guilty about her reaction, it had become so strong and negative that she was sure she'd go crazy unless they split up.

Why Are We So Annoying?

When was the last time your spouse did something that annoyed you? Last week? Yesterday? An hour ago? If you're male, the answer is probably "last week." If you're female, it's more likely to be "this very minute."

For some yet unknown reason, women seem to find men more annoying than men find women. But, male or female, our annoying habits draw love units out of our spouse's Love Bank every time.

As a marriage counselor, I tell couples that eliminating annoying behavior will improve their marriages. This is not rocket science. It only makes sense that you'll get along better if you stop doing things that drive each other to distraction. But you'd be amazed how many couples just don't get it.

"If George loved me, he'd let our cats sleep with us at night," says one wife—and poor George is sitting next to her, rolling his sleep-deprived eyes.

"If Ellen just accepted me for who I am," a husband says, "she wouldn't mind the T-shirts I wear around the house."

"The torn T-shirts," Ellen adds. "The torn, stained T-shirts. The torn, stained T-shirts two sizes too small."

Couples sit in my office and try to convince me that they should be able to do whatever they please—the objecting spouse should adjust to the annoying behavior.

Of course, when *we're* annoyed, we usually think others are being inconsiderate, particularly when we've explained how it bothers us and they continue to do it. But when our behavior annoys *others,* we feel we have a right to persist, demanding that others adjust to us.

I often wish I could switch a couple's minds: Joe becomes Jane for a day and Jane becomes Joe. If they could only know *how* annoying their habits are, surely they would try to become more considerate.

Part of the reason we're insensitive to the feelings of others is that we don't feel what they feel. As a counselor, I try to help couples become more empathetic—see situations through each other's eyes.

In *A Christmas Carol,* Scrooge is guided by the ghosts of Christmas into the lives of people he has hurt. He witnesses firsthand the effect of his greed on the life of the Cratchit family, particularly Tiny Tim. His exposure to their pain helps transform him into a more caring human being.

I wish we all had "ghosts" that would help us see how we affect others, particularly the ones we care for the most. I think we would tend to respond the way Scrooge did—with greater sensitivity and consideration.

Our Annoying Habits

I've found it helpful to divide annoying behavior into two categories. If it's repeated without much thought, I call it an annoying *habit.* If it's usually scheduled and requires thought to complete, I call it an annoying *activity.*

Personal mannerisms such as the way you eat, the way you clean up after yourself, and the way you talk are possible examples of annoying habits. Annoying activities, on the other hand, may include sporting events you attend, your choice of church, and a personal exercise program.

Annoying habits are not necessarily a part of your character or identity. Many of them develop randomly, over time, for trivial reasons. Some parents raise their children to be considerate, and others leave the development of habits to chance. Unfortunately chance is not a considerate teacher, and many people are stuck with a spouse who never learned basic social skills.

I've been impressed with how these people can clean up their act after marriage. The positive influence of their spouse helps them become more socially sensitive. They change their behavior to please their spouse, but these changes also make them more acceptable in general society.

Some habits are relatively easy to overcome. For example, if a woman is disgusted with her husband's personal hygiene, he can learn, without much difficulty, to shave, shower, and wash his hair daily, brush his teeth at least twice a day, and wear clean clothes.

Other characteristically male habits, such as spitting on the sidewalk, using coarse language, and telling offensive jokes, are more difficult to overcome. But once a man commits to ridding himself of these habits, he can usually avoid them entirely, at least when he's with his wife.

Mike's annoying habits had become a barrier to his effort to meet Sharon's emotional needs. They were so distracting and irritating to her that she didn't want to be affectionate, make love to him, or even talk to him. So not only did he *lose* love units, but the habits also prevented him from *depositing* love units. It wasn't that he didn't know how to meet her emotional needs—he was capable when he had a chance. But his annoying habits had not given him a chance.

Indulging in Annoying Activities

Gwen should have seen it coming. When she and John were dating, he always chose what they did. Either she joined him or he'd go without her.

The pattern continued during the first few years of marriage. John went fishing, played basketball with friends, and attended sporting events or watched them on TV. Gwen was welcome to come along but she didn't enjoy any of those activities.

"John, why do you insist on doing things I don't like?" she finally asked. "Can't we do things together that I enjoy too?"

"Like shopping?"

Gwen's face fell, and John knew he'd hurt her feelings.

"I'm sorry, Gwen. I didn't mean to upset you. But we just don't go for the same things. You have your interests, and I have mine. There's nothing wrong with that."

If there was nothing wrong with it, why did it bother Gwen so much?

While he watched *Monday Night Football,* she watched another program in their bedroom. She tried to develop an interest in football and watch it with him but she simply found it too boring. Watching him play basketball on Wednesday wasn't her idea of a great time either. She went fishing with him some weekends but she couldn't handle deer hunting. And sometimes she wasn't even invited to some of the sporting events he attended with his friends.

There was nothing illegal or immoral about John's choice of activities. But whenever he chose to do one of them, he was not taking Gwen's feelings into account, and *that's* what was wrong.

It seemed to Gwen that John was married to his sporting events rather than to her, and she resented it. Every time John went off on his own, he depleted his account in Gwen's Love Bank. She began to withdraw from him emotionally, looking for activities to do on her own. Fortunately they came to me for counseling before she withdrew entirely.

Getting through to John was a major struggle. He seemed almost addicted to his recreational activities. I could see why Gwen had been almost ready to give up. We went over and over the fact that what he did wasn't wrong in itself—he hadn't done it to annoy Gwen—but it *did* annoy her. He kept arguing that if she was annoyed, it was her problem. I kept insisting that it was *their* problem, and he had to assume responsibility for how his behavior affected her.

The notion that he was partially responsible for her emotional reactions caught him by surprise. He never quite understood how love worked. He thought it had something to do with "chemistry" and that if people were right for each other they'd simply "feel" it. He didn't understand what he had done to build enough love units for Gwen to marry him and he didn't understand what he was doing now to destroy that love.

Getting Rid of Annoying Behavior

Annoying habits and activities are Love Busters, destroyers of romantic love. A single destructive act is bad enough, but a destructive marital habit is repeated over and over, multiplying the destruction and withdrawing love units repeatedly and insidiously.

Most of our behavior is habitual. We may think we act spontaneously and originally, but on closer analysis, we tend to be very predictable. We have the power to change and we can turn destructive habits into constructive ones if we have a good reason to do so. But once a destructive marital habit is in place, it can spell doom for the relationship. It's like a crack in the dam. Unless you repair it, it gets bigger and bigger, until all of the water eventually escapes.

Since annoying behavior is more characteristic of men than women, some of my clients have seen it as a male characteristic that women must learn to endure. Men tend to have inherently disgusting habits, they argue, and their favorite activities cannot usually be shared or even understood by most women. Many men don't even consider giving up their annoying habits and activities—that would place them in submission to women, threatening their essential manliness, they maintain.

But this issue has nothing to do with personal characteristics, manliness, or power struggles. We are dealing with the simple issue of *consideration*. If a man wants to live with a woman, it makes sense for him to take her feelings into account. I don't ask men to sacrifice their manliness. I simply want them to avoid gaining pleasure at the expense of their wife. The following steps will help a couple get rid of annoying behaviors.

Step 1: Make a commitment.

The first step is simply to decide to do something. Decide *together* that you must become considerate toward each other. Although the will to change is the easiest part of the process and does not in any way guarantee a successful result, it is still essential. Without this decision, there's no point in continuing.

To verify this willingness to change, I usually have each individual sign the following agreement, a commitment to avoid inconsiderate behavior.

Agreement to Overcome Annoying Behavior

This Agreement is made this _____ day of _____ , 19___ , between _____ , hereinafter called "husband," and _____ , hereinafter called "wife," whereby it is mutually agreed:

The husband and wife agree to avoid being the cause of each other's pain or discomfort by protecting each other from their annoying habits and activities. They will follow a course of action that identifies their annoying behavior, investigates the motives and causes of the behavior, and eliminates the behavior.

In Witness Whereof, the parties hereto have signed this agreement on the day and year first above written.

_____   _____
Husband's Signature   Wife's Signature

Step 2: Identify the Love Busters.

After a husband and wife agree to become more considerate, they must identify annoying habits and activities. They do this by making a list of each other's behavior that annoys them. Beside each entry, I ask them to put a number between 1 and 10, indicating how intensely they are annoyed (1 = mildly annoying, 10 = extremely annoying). The numbers help identify the behavior that is withdrawing the most love units.

The wife's list is almost always longer than the husband's list. In fact for many couples I counsel, the husbands have no entries at all, but it's not uncommon for a woman to list more than fifty habits and activities she finds annoying.

I assure these husbands that a long list of irritating behaviors should not lead them to conclude that there is no hope. The list is a first step toward resolving problems that have been swept under a rug. They must uncover the dirt before they can vacuum it up.

Step 3: Eliminate the easy ones first.

In most cases, a list of annoying behaviors will include a few that a spouse can easily overcome. For example, consider the following list of annoying behaviors with the ratings given by one wife.

Intensity Rating	Annoying Behavior
4	Complains too much about work
5	Doesn't clean the bathroom after getting ready in the morning
3	Doesn't hang up his clothes when he gets ready for bed
5	Watches too much TV
7	Snacks too much
6	Drinks too much pop

Intensity Rating	Annoying Behavior
10	Chews ice and spits it back into the glass
10	Licks his knife at the dinner table
7	His feet smell; he needs to bathe more often
7	He is overweight; he eats too much

Some of these annoying behaviors are very easy to overcome, while others are very difficult. To shorten the list with relatively little effort, I ask the annoying spouse to look it over and check off those behaviors that he or she can eliminate with little effort. In this case, the husband may agree to stop complaining about work when he comes home every night. He may also agree to clean up the bathroom after he uses it in the morning and hang up his clothes when he gets ready for bed.

Very often a commitment made in my office to eliminate some of these annoying habits is all it takes. From that moment on, those problems are things of the past. Of course, if a few weeks later they pop up again, we simply put them back on the list of behaviors to overcome.

Step 4: Select three Love Busters to overcome.

Now that our list of annoying behaviors is down to seven, should the couple work on all of them at once? I don't recommend it. I suggest that a couple focus on the three annoyances that get the highest intensity ratings. If more than three have the highest rating, I have the annoyed spouse select the three that are most important to overcome.

On the list above, there are two 10s—chewing ice and spitting it back into the glass and licking his knife at the dinner table. Since there are three tied for 7—the next highest intensity rating—the spouse must pick just one of these to make three. Suppose the wife who made the list chooses "eats too much" as the most important to her from the three choices. That choice leaves four on the original list that will be addressed at a later time.

Step 5: Why is the Love Buster there in the first place?

After three annoying habits or activities have been selected, we're ready for the next step. We need to know why the behavior formed and what's keeping it there. I use the following questionnaire to help a couple investigate the background of each behavior.

The purpose of each question is fairly self-explanatory. Not only do I want a couple to understand the background of the behavior, but I want them to think it through as well. Most spouses engage in

Annoying Behavior Questionnaire

All the following questions apply to this annoying behavior:

1. When did you begin to engage in this behavior?
2. What are the most important reasons that you began?
3. What are the most important reasons that you engage in this behavior now?
4. When you engage in this behavior, how do you feel?
5. When you engage in this behavior, how does your spouse feel?
6. If you have ever tried to avoid this behavior, how did you do it?
7. If you decided to avoid this behavior entirely, would you be successful?
8. Are you willing to avoid this behavior?
9. Do you have any suggestions that would make the elimination of this behavior more likely?

annoying behavior because they enjoy the activity. They may give a more philosophical explanation but deep down they know that it simply feels good to be doing what they do.

For example, some clients explain that jogging, body building, aerobic exercise, and biking are necessary to sustain their health. But they carry their activities to such an extreme that they dominate and interfere with their spouse's life. The truth is they enjoy their exercise so much that they can't seem to get enough of it. When their spouse complains, they often refuse to negotiate the issue.

Once in a while, I find a client who engages in an annoying activity purely on principle. He or she seems to gain no pleasure but does it with missionary zeal. Then there are people who have compulsive emotional disorders and they persist in repetitive activities due to the disorder. But whatever the reason for the annoying activity, my goal is to help the client overcome it or negotiate a compromise that makes it acceptable.

Step 6: Create a plan to overcome the Love Buster.

If a person does not gain much pleasure from the annoying behavior, it is relatively easy to abandon or modify the behavior. However, if the pleasure is intense, if the reasons are embedded in his or her sense of morality, or if the behavior is caused by emotional disorders, overcoming the behavior can be a major project.

The annoying behaviors selected above exist because the husband enjoys doing them. He enjoys leaving the bathroom a mess in the morning and he enjoys leaving his clothes out at night. But what he enjoys the most is eating. So "eating too much" will be the most difficult to overcome.

The plan to clean up the bathroom and pick up his clothes may not require much strategy, but it *will* require a definition of what constitutes a clean bathroom and picked-up clothes.

The plan to eat less requires much more thought and planning. After all, to eat less means the husband will suffer through every day unless he and his wife can think of a way to curb his appetite.

The annoying behavior questionnaire helps create an effective plan because it addresses many of the obstacles. Unless obstacles, like a voracious appetite, are considered, a plan will not be successful.

Step 7: Measure your progress.

Whether a plan is easy or difficult to implement, it helps to document your progress. I encourage couples I counsel to keep track of how things are going by writing any instance of annoying behavior on a sheet of paper. The date, time, and circumstances should also be documented. The spouse who finds the behavior annoying should keep the record.

If a plan is followed perfectly, there is nothing to document. Only instances of failure need to be noted. When couples come for counseling, they bring the progress report with them, and we discuss every failure. If the plan is not proving successful in eliminating the annoying behaviors, we change the plan.

In completing this report, honesty is essential. All too often, in an effort to be helpful, the annoyed spouse goes easy on the mate and underreports annoying incidents. This gives a false impression of success, which can undermine the entire process.

Over a period of several weeks, the frequency of reported failure usually drops to almost zero. Since I often work on three annoying behaviors at a time, attention may shift to one of the three that is more resistant to change. But eventually all three are usually overcome. At this point another three annoying behaviors can be focused on, and the process can begin again. Or the couple may decide that the first three were the only ones necessary to change.

I don't consider the behavior overcome until at least three months have passed with no failure. A phenomenon called "spontaneous recovery" can sometimes cause the behavior to mysteriously reappear months or even years after it seemed to end. But in such recurrences, the behavior is no longer a well-formed habit and can usually be overcome without much effort.

Here I've regarded annoying behavior as essentially unintentional. Intentionally annoying behavior usually falls into the category of anger, which we covered in chapter 2. But whether or not your behavior is intentionally annoying, the outcome is the same—love units are lost. Sometimes it's more difficult to eliminate annoying behavior than angry outbursts or disrespectful judgments because people feel that it's their intentions that matter. That line of thinking can get a marriage into serious trouble.

Replace Love Busters with Love Builders

If you simply eliminate your enjoyable activities and find no replacement, you'll either become very depressed or revert to the activities you left. But if you replace them with activities your spouse can enjoy with you, you win the prize of romantic love.

In my book *His Needs, Her Needs,* I offer suggestions for developing mutually enjoyable activities in chapter 6 on recreational companionship. Why waste precious time enjoying activities apart from each other when you could be enjoying them together? Think of the love units you could be depositing!

Marriages usually go one of two ways: Nature takes its course and marital compatibility is eventually lost, or a couple can decide to build compatibility by eliminating annoying behavior and replacing it with behavior that meets emotional needs. My years of marriage counseling have taught me a very important lesson: *Marital compatibility is created.*

When couples divorce or separate because they're "incompatible," does this mean they were doomed from the start? Is there some basic personality clash they just can't overcome? No, it just means they've been ineffective in *creating compatibility.* Very likely they developed interests and activities independently of each other. They weren't thoughtful enough to try to include each other in the most enjoyable moments of their lives.

What a shame! It didn't have to be that way. Their marriage, their family, and in many cases, their happiness could have been saved if only they had used a little thought and consideration.

That doesn't mean just giving your spouse a chance to join you in activities *you* find enjoyable. It means searching for activities of *mutual* enjoyment until they're found. It means replacing activities that have come between you with activities that bring you together.

Selfish Demands 5

Who Wants to Live with a Dictator?

andy learned a simple rule from his parents: *If you want something, demand it!* Oh, they never put it in so many words, but Randy would hear his mother shout orders to his father, and his father would reluctantly obey. Once in a while, his father would get what he needed by ordering Randy's mother around.

Randy's wife, Jane, had an almost identical background. She too learned the point-and-shoot method of problem solving from her parents. "Do this! Get me that! I need it!" The fact that both Randy's and Jane's parents were eventually divorced did not prevent their children from adopting this family tradition.

When they were first married, their tendency to demand their way did not surface very often. Randy and Jane were very much in love. If Randy wanted something of Jane, he would only have to ask, and she would usually accommodate him. If he sensed any reluctance, he would assume that she would help him later, and he'd withdraw his request. Jane did the same. Their uncomplicated lives and their eagerness to make each other happy kept selfish demands to a minimum.

The baby changed everything. When little Christine arrived, both parents struggled to keep up with their new responsibilities. This stretched their ability to care for each other and they reverted to habits they learned from their parents.

"Randy, would you please help me with the laundry? I won't have time to do it today."

"Honey, I'm sorry, but I've absolutely caved in. I'm so tired that I can't think straight."

"What about me? You think I'm well rested? I have an exhausting job too! You get up right now and help me—or else!"

"Or else what?"

"Do you really want to find out?"

Randy didn't want to find out, so he got up and did the laundry. Besides, he knew Jane was tired and he didn't blame her for threatening him.

From Jane's perspective, it worked great. All she had to do was demand help, and Randy responded. Jane's mother must have known what she was doing all along!

The pattern continued over the next few months. Whenever Randy came home from work exhausted and he balked at sharing household chores, Jane would simply order him to help. He helped her, but each time she gained at his expense—and her account in his Love Bank lost a few love units. Worse yet, she was training *him* to use the same Love Buster.

When children arrive and life suddenly seems overwhelming and exhausting, one area in marriage that often suffers is sexual fulfillment. Before Christine came along, Randy and Jane had a very active and satisfying sexual relationship. But after the baby was born, Jane did not feel like making love as often. She was simply too tired most of the time, and Christine interfered with their privacy.

As you might guess, this frustrated Randy. Night after night, he found his amorous advances halted as Jane rolled over and went to sleep. He was finally turned down once too often and decided to try

Jane's strategy: He *ordered* her to make love to him—or else. If she refused, he'd have to find someone else. Horrified by his threat, Jane reluctantly consented.

The sex was not great for either of them but it seemed to solve Randy's problem. When it was over, Jane cried, but now it was Randy who rolled over and went to sleep.

From that day on, their sexual relationship changed. Instead of mutual agreement and satisfaction, they had sex on demand. Whenever Randy insisted on sex, Jane obliged. She rarely enjoyed it and eventually came to hate it.

Housework on demand withdrew a few love units from Jane's account in Randy's Love Bank. But sex on demand withdrew a gigantic sum of love units from Randy's account with Jane. It eventually destroyed her feelings of romantic love for him.

Demands Create Resentment

We've all experienced demands. Our parents made demands on us when we were children, teachers made demands in school, and employers sometimes make demands at work. Most of us didn't like them as children and we still don't.

Demands imply a threat of punishment—an "or else." Sometimes the threat isn't stated, but it's there. Jane's "or else" became a promise of unspecified punishment. "Do you really want to know?" Randy spelled out his threat in horrifying detail—he would find someone else to sleep with. No matter how specific, the threat conveys a message: "If you refuse, you'll regret it. You may dislike doing what I want but if you don't do it, I'll make sure you suffer even greater pain."

But it doesn't end there. The threatened spouse often refuses to grant the demand, forcing a test of power. If the demanding partner lacks the power to follow through with the threat, he or she often receives punishment, or at least ridicule, for making empty threats. Sometimes the one on the receiving end of the demand may issue a counterthreat—Jane might say, "If you sleep with someone else, I'll divorce you and sue you for every cent you have."

Whenever a demand is made, the one meeting the demand will feel a certain resentment. But if a power struggle ensues, the loser will feel a much deeper resentment, and the winner may also be battle scarred.

What's wrong with asking for what you want? Nothing. But when one spouse demands something, he or she is ignoring the feelings of the other spouse. Worse yet, a demand is a way of saying, "I want you to suffer so I can have my way."

Some might ask, "But what if she lies around the house all day? What if he goes out with his friends every night, leaving me with the kids? What if she makes no effort to do anything for me? What then?"

I'd say you have a serious problem. But demands will not solve it. If you force your spouse to meet your needs, it becomes a temporary solution at best, and resentment is sure to be the cost. Either meet each other's needs willingly, from a commitment of mutual care, or do not meet them at all. Threats, lectures, and other forms of manipulation do not build compatibility—they build resentment.

Those who make demands play a zero-sum game—the gains of the winning player equal the losses of the losing player. A marriage cannot endure zero-sum games. Gaining at your spouse's expense depletes your Love Bank account and destroys romantic love. Even if you win this time, you lose in the long run. The Policy of Joint Agreement—*Never do anything without an enthusiastic agreement between you and your spouse*—guards against zero-sum games. It will not let you make selfish demands.

The Policy would have preserved Jane's love for Randy. If he had asked her how she felt about having sex with him on a particular night, she would have told him she was too tired. He would then have withdrawn the request, and none of Jane's love for him would have been lost. They would not have made love that night, but their romantic love would have been secure. And with romantic love, all marital problems (including sexual ones) are much easier to solve.

But Randy demanded sex and each time he did, Jane loved him less. Eventually she didn't love him at all and refused to have sex with him. When he threatened to have an affair, she told him to go right ahead. After six months of sexual abstinence, they came to me for counseling.

Randy had not understood how fragile their love was. He also didn't understand how important love had been in getting his demands met. When Jane was in love, she wanted to make Randy happy, and his demands provided a little extra shove. But when her love was gone, she deeply resented his demands, so she simply refused them.

When his demands were refused, he launched a threat—"I'll find someone else." When Jane said, "Go right ahead," Randy had a tough choice: make good on the threat by finding another woman for sex or admit his threat was without teeth. He wisely opted for the latter.

What would Jane have done if Randy had chosen to have an affair? I don't know—but it certainly would not have endeared him to her. She might have tried to give their sexual relationship one last shot, just to save the marriage. But any improvement in their sexual relationship would have been temporary at best, since his affair would have withdrawn even more love units from Jane's already depleted Love Bank. Sooner or later she would hate him so much that she couldn't stand the sight of him.

The long-term solution to their crisis was simply this: *Abandon selfish demands.*

A year earlier Randy had begun making demands on Jane sexually because it seemed to be the only way to avoid a life of celibacy. But now he could see that his demands had also led to celibacy. There had to be another solution, and he was ready for suggestions.

I reminded him that the best sexual relationship he'd ever had with Jane was not motivated by demands but by love. Once he stopped threatening her and began depositing love units, her love for him would be restored and his sexual need would be much easier for her to meet.

When one spouse hurts the other in some way, it's common for the injured spouse to withdraw emotionally. It's a self-defense mechanism. Emotional withdrawal protects your nearly empty Love Bank from further depletion but it also makes it difficult for the other spouse to reverse the cycle and start *depositing* love units. By the time they came to see me, Jane had clearly withdrawn. Randy would have to prove he would not hurt her before she would trust him with her deepest emotions again.

He agreed to eliminate all demands. He would have sex with Jane only when she was enthusiastically willing. It took several months for that day to arrive because so many love units needed to be redeposited in her Love Bank. But when they started to make love again, it had the quality they'd experienced in the early years of marriage. Eventually he was satisfied with the frequency of their lovemaking as well.

Demands serve a shortsighted purpose: forcing a spouse to care when the spouse is unwilling. When Randy married Jane, promising to be faithful to her, he assumed that she was agreeing to meet his sexual needs. (Without such an implicit agreement, why else would he have agreed to an exclusive sexual relationship?) So when Jane didn't fulfill her "marital obligation," he felt he had the right to force her to keep her part of the bargain. That tactic may work in labor negotiations but not in a marriage based on love. Sex has to be more than a "marital obligation."

Of course, when she took her wedding vow, Jane hadn't said anything about meeting his sexual needs. Most couples assume, rightly or wrongly, that they will be so in love with each other that sex will be frequent and wonderful. So there's no need to spell that out in advance. They don't think in terms of "obligations."

But as the marriage wears on, and often after children enter the family, sex becomes more difficult to enjoy, to schedule, to stay awake for. In such times, a couple can get seriously out of sync. What do you do when one wants sex and the other doesn't? It's suddenly easy to start thinking about obligations. "You owe me . . . You promised . . . Give me what I want or else."

But it doesn't work.

By withdrawing love units, demands destroy the very feelings of love you need to enjoy sex. It's a bit like a football coach barking at his nervous young quarterback, "You've got to relax out there! Relax or I'm yanking you from the game!" How can the kid relax when the coach is threatening him? The same thing happens with demands in a marriage: You're asking your spouse to show love to you (whether by making love or drying the dishes) but the way you're asking destroys that same love. How can your mate show you love when your behavior is ruining it?

Even with his sexual fulfillment at risk, Randy could not afford to sacrifice Jane's feelings for him. He needed to solve his sexual problem in a way that preserved her feeling of love for him.

Habits are formed when behavior is rewarded. The way to encourage your spouse to make love more often is to make lovemaking an enjoyable experience. If lovemaking is unpleasant, your spouse will do the predictable thing—avoid it next time. When your husband or wife is too tired or sick or just not in the mood, you take a big risk by insisting on sex. The next time it will be that much more difficult to make love.

If sex is often unpleasant for your spouse, he or she may refuse to have sex with you altogether. To avoid that unhappy outcome, never demand it! If you've made no demands, and you're dissatisfied with the quantity or quality of your sexual experience, you're ready to make a *thoughtful request*.

Turning Selfish Demands into Thoughtful Requests

People feel used when you show no consideration for their feelings. Even when they've agreed to help you in return for your help, they can still come away feeling resentful if you do something that makes their effort unpleasant. So as you consider asking your spouse for help, be concerned about how he or she will feel about it. The best way to find out is to ask.

Step 1: Explain what you want and ask how your spouse feels about it.

This first step makes all the difference in the world. Suddenly the focus is not just on *what you want,* but also on *how your partner feels.* That's considerate; that's thoughtful. Now your spouse doesn't feel taken for granted. You have shown that his or her feelings matter to you.

In many cases, the thoughtful request itself will make your mate want to do what you've asked. Your concern for his or her feelings deposits love units, and your spouse will want to make you happy. Besides, just knowing that you care makes the task more enjoyable.

Bask in this bliss for a moment because it isn't always that simple. If thoughtful requests produced instant agreement, most of us would have given up demands long ago. Sometimes a spouse still finds the request unpleasant to fulfill. What then?

Step 2: If your spouse has a problem with your request, withdraw it.

Thoughtfulness is more than how you ask for something. If you really care about your spouse's feelings (as your thoughtful request indicates you do), you want him or her to *enjoy* doing what you've asked. You will not take "well, all right, I guess" for an answer. If your spouse balks at helping you, withdraw the request.

This second step will not be taken by anyone who believes his or her spouse owes favors, has a duty to meet needs, or must do what he or she is told.

In counseling some couples, I first must convince them that they do not have the *right* to make demands of each other. Indeed, some assume that their wedding vows gave them this right. But we have already seen how demands choke the feelings of love. Let me add that selfish demands are basically immoral. We do not have the right to gain at someone else's expense, and that's what demands are all about.

Being considerate is not just a word game. It means behaving in a way that takes other people's feelings into account. If you suspect that your spouse will find it unpleasant to meet your request, you're thoughtless if you persist.

This leaves many people in a quandary. They do not want to be thoughtless, but how will their basic emotional needs be met?

I've encountered a few people who simply refuse to do anything for their spouse unless they're threatened with abandonment or some other punishment. They suffer from a pervasive character disorder that limits their ability to care for others. Even in these cases, demands do not solve the problem for the long term.

Fortunately, in the vast majority of couples I've seen, reciprocal care is instinctive, and demands are unnecessary if requests are made thoughtfully. With this in mind, I encourage couples to take one final step when a request has been rejected and withdrawn.

Step 3: Discuss other ways your spouse could enthusiastically help you.

If your marriage is healthy, your spouse probably wants to help you—even if he or she is uncomfortable with your request. The problem is often with the *way* you want your spouse to meet your need.

For example, if Randy wants Jane to help him clean out the garage, she may object because of his timing. Suppose she's been looking forward to spending that time on another project that's more important to her. After she declines his initial request, he may ask if she would be willing to help at some other time. It may turn out that she doesn't mind helping him the following weekend.

But what if she can't imagine *ever* helping with the garage? What if Jane sees that as Randy's job, and his alone?

This is where the Policy of Joint Agreement gets a workout. Randy must not demand his way, even if he is demanding an alternative to his original request. He needs to approach this discussion seeking a solution to which Jane will enthusiastically agree. Together they can brainstorm the situation, looking for arrangements that will satisfy them both. If they cannot find a way for Jane to be enthusiastic about cleaning the garage, Randy should drop the issue—not grudgingly but out of love for his wife. (Similarly he would want her to drop requests that he can't become enthusiastic about.)

Randy may never get help in cleaning the garage, but there are far more important issues at stake here. By engaging in the process of thoughtful requests and the negotiations that follow, he is building up his account in Jane's Love Bank, ensuring that his most important emotional needs will be met. And how important is a garage, really, compared to a love that grows between a husband and wife?

Thoughtful Requests Build Habits

Ultimately you want to receive help without even having to ask. In other words, you want your spouse to form the *habit* of helping you (as you develop a habit of helping your spouse). Demands cannot accomplish this. Demands may get the job done in the present but they sabotage the future.

Habits form when you repeatedly find pleasure in doing certain things. When you make a thoughtful request, you set up the necessary conditions for habit formation. Your spouse feels good knowing that you care for his or her feelings, and you care enough to withdraw your request if necessary. Your spouse should also find pleasure in knowing that he or she can do something to make you happy—when you work together to find a mutually enjoyable way to meet your need. With these pleasurable feelings involved, and free from the discomfort of demands, a habit can begin to form as your spouse acts on your request.

Do you want to go through the rest of your life reminding your spouse of everything you want and need? You can avoid all that simply by being thoughtful and thus building need-meeting habits in both you and your spouse.

Thoughtfulness is constructive. Selfishness is destructive.

Dishonesty 6

Who Wants to Live with a Liar?

Jennifer found it easy to be honest with Ed about her feelings—while they were dating. He was a great guy, always trying to meet her needs, so her accolades far outweighed her complaints. On the few occasions when he did something to upset her, she mentioned it briefly, and he quickly made accommodations.

The first time Jennifer was dishonest with Ed about her feelings was during their honeymoon. They were having dinner together in a restaurant that was right on the beach. The evening was beautiful and from where they were seated, they could watch the waves crashing onto the sand.

Then Ed's cellular phone rang, and the mood suddenly changed. Ed had given his number to some of his best customers and one of them wanted help with a problem.

Ed excused himself to talk to his customer, leaving Jennifer to enjoy the scenery and her dinner—alone. Half an hour later Ed returned, with apologies for the interruption.

Though Jennifer was deeply offended by the way Ed had treated her, she did not tell him how bad she felt. Instead, she told him how much she was enjoying the scenery.

That call at dinner was not the only one that interrupted their honeymoon. Ed received several calls, once while he and Jennifer were making love. Jennifer was hurt that Ed was trying to conduct business during their honeymoon but she never let him know. She wanted him to be successful in his business and felt she had to learn to adjust.

Because of his demanding job, Ed left Jennifer alone three nights each week. This bothered her but she didn't want him to worry, so she let him think she felt happy with the arrangement.

Then they had children. With all the fuss of caring for little ones, both Ed and Jennifer became increasingly distracted. The marriage became a source of dissatisfaction and disappointment, but neither Ed nor Jennifer thought it right to complain. Each knew the other worked hard and tried to do his or her best. The dishonesty was now mutual and growing.

Ed felt unfulfilled with their sexual relationship but he understood the pressure Jennifer was under. After a long day of child care, of course she'd be tired when he came home from work late at night! He just couldn't expect her to meet his sexual needs whenever he felt amorous. So he didn't tell her about his increasing sexual frustration.

Jennifer was not *totally* silent about her feelings. Once in a great while, when he came home after another late night at the office, she'd say, "I'm feeling lonely."

Ed would react a little defensively, "Well, I don't know how we can pay these bills if I don't work."

"Yeah, I guess you're right." Jennifer would drop the subject and Ed would think she was satisfied with his answer. But she wasn't. She had told him how she felt, and he didn't seem to care.

And Ed even told Jennifer how he felt about their sexual relationship—once. When Jennifer explained that the children made her too tired at night, he said he understood. And he did, but the problem still bothered him.

Meanwhile, both Ed and Jennifer were innocently creating incompatibility. Love Busters were sprouting like weeds because neither one said anything when his or her interests were neglected. They were not meeting each other's emotional needs for the same reason, because neither one complained. Before long they were no longer in love with each other.

Types of Dishonesty

There are three reasons for dishonesty in marriage: (1) protection, (2) avoiding trouble, and (3) compulsion. While the motives, and excuses, are very different for each type, the result is the same—the marriage suffers.

Lying to Protect

Jennifer and Ed were practicing the first goal of dishonesty—protection. They were really trying to care for each other, to protect each other from the pain of criticism. In other cases, people protect their spouses from unpleasant information, perhaps a health scare or a financial setback. I call these people "protector liars" and most of us fit this category, at least once in a while. Almost everybody can think of times when they have withheld their true feelings to avoid upsetting their spouse.

It seems quite innocent, doesn't it? The problem with protective lying is that it does far more than protect—it *denies* a spouse crucial information. As Ed and Jennifer protected each other from the truth about their feelings, they were both making huge withdrawals of love units *without knowing it*. Ed's work schedule was siphoning love units out of Jennifer's Love Bank, but she wasn't saying anything about it. Each time Jennifer turned down Ed's sexual advances, she was withdrawing from her account in Ed's Love Bank, but he pretended there was nothing wrong.

How would you feel if your bank stopped giving you monthly statements on your checking account but continued to deduct fees without informing you? You'd be outraged. "When our customers run low in their accounts," the bank manager might say, "we try to protect them from that unpleasant information." It's crazy! That's exactly the time you *need* information, so you can make some deposits and avoid bouncing checks.

The same is true of Jennifer and Ed. If they had known how often they were withdrawing love units, they could have made adjustments to prevent further losses. But without that information, they were blindly drifting into incompatibility.

Lying to Avoid Trouble

Avoiding trouble is the second goal of dishonesty, arising from the threat of being caught doing something wrong. What is right and wrong, of course, is often in the eyes of the beholder, so "avoiding-trouble liars" often try to justify their own shady actions but they know that others will judge them harshly. In marriage, these people do things they know their spouse disapproves of, but to avoid their spouse's judgment, they lie.

Sally is an example of the avoiding-trouble liar. Always short of cash, she hated begging Steve, her husband, for money. So Sally opened her own bank account by forging her husband's signature on a ten-thousand-dollar loan application. She planned to make the payments with the money she earned working part-time. Steve suspected that something was going on, but Sally adamantly denied any wrongdoing.

Sally's plan might have gone undetected if she hadn't spent all the money and then missed a payment on the loan. When Steve got a call from the bank, the cat was out of the bag.

"None of this would have happened if Steve hadn't been so cheap" was her excuse. According to Sally, she had a right to spend more money than Steve gave her, and so she took matters into her own hands. She justified her dishonesty as necessary for her survival.

People who have affairs often feel the same way. With their spouses unwilling to meet their needs, they are "forced" to find another who is willing. Most people caught in affairs are more upset about the fact that they were caught than they are about the pain they've caused their spouse and children. While admitting that they hurt their spouse, very few actually feel guilty about it. If their spouse had met their needs in the first place, they figure, none of it would have happened.

These people don't lie because they're *ashamed* of their actions; lying is just a necessary part of the process. Since the spouse would not understand or accept the truth and would certainly cause a great deal of trouble, these liars simply avoid trouble by covering up their illicit deeds. Ironically, when caught in a lie, an avoiding-trouble liar will often keep lying to get out of the trouble *that* causes. When these lies don't work, the person tries to avoid trouble by dodging responsibility. "I wouldn't have to lie if you'd just mind your own business."

Born Liars

The third type of dishonesty is compulsion. Some people lie about anything and everything, whether they have a good reason or not. I call them "born liars." They don't seem to be able to control it nor do they know why they do it. These people start lying from the time they can first talk. They often lie about personal experiences and accomplishments and sometimes even convince themselves that the lies are true. Even evidence to the contrary does not always dissuade them.

Born liars often live double lives. Occasionally you'll read a news story about some con artist who has finally been caught; often these are born liars—passing themselves off as doctors or lawyers or marrying two or more people. When caught red-handed in a crime, they sincerely deny any involvement and can even pass lie detector tests. Such liars are fascinating to psychologists such as myself, but for obvious reasons they're impossible as marriage partners. Since honesty is essential in marriage, and these individuals simply cannot tell the truth, their marriages are usually very short-lived.

This third category, compulsion, is obviously the most severe form of dishonesty, and thankfully, very few of the spouses I counsel are born liars. If you and your spouse are dealing with dishonesty, it's probably protective lying or avoiding-trouble lying. Though less severe, either of these can do major damage to a marriage. Fortunately, however, the pattern of dishonesty can be changed.

Is Honesty a Love Buster?

Isn't *honesty,* in some cases, a Love Buster? Aren't there times when a couple can be *too* honest with each other, when it would be better to avoid conflict by keeping a spouse in the dark?

That's what Ed and Jennifer thought. They assumed their relationship would suffer harm if they expressed their true feelings. And on the surface, this argument seems to make sense. Love Busters are those actions that make your spouse unhappy; so if your expression of honesty troubles your spouse, it's a Love Buster.

Not so fast. When you take a closer look, you find that the Love Buster isn't honesty itself, but the thing that honesty reveals. Confessing to an affair will certainly upset your spouse, but it isn't the confession that's upsetting. It's the affair!

In most cases, dishonesty merely postpones your spouse's discovery of the truth, and once it's revealed, the fact that you lied will do even more damage to your relationship. Then your spouse will be upset by the truth *and* your dishonesty. And of the two, your dishonesty will usually hurt your spouse more than whatever it was you were trying to conceal. Dishonesty in marriage, once discovered, causes incredible pain.

Don't Wrap Your Honesty in Love Busters

Can your expression of honesty actually be a Love Buster in disguise? What if Jennifer had greeted Ed at the door by throwing a dish at him? "You never have time for me anymore, you selfish jerk!

I don't know why I ever married you!" All right, she gets points for honesty, but her angry outburst ruins it all. Ed will never hear the genuine feelings she is expressing, because he's running for cover.

Or, after Ed defends his need to earn a living for the family, suppose Jennifer says, "That's all you ever think about—money, money, money. Your priorities sure are screwed up." That may be her honest opinion, but she's wrapping it in a disrespectful judgment, which forces Ed to defend his priorities. As he tries to support his own position, he never really hears what Jennifer is saying. Whatever gain she gets from expressing her feelings is quickly nullified by the Love Buster.

We've seen another husband demanding sex from his wife. What if Ed chose that approach, trying to end his frustration by making a selfish demand of Jennifer? There's nothing wrong with his honest appeal for her help but when he turns it into a demand, it's a Love Buster.

Many people wrap their honest feelings in the poison of Love Busters. When havoc results, they go back to bottling up their feelings. "I tried being honest and look where it got me." It's not easy expressing honest feelings without angry outbursts, disrespectful judgments, or selfish demands, but anyone can learn to do it.

"I'm the least important person in your life; you'd rather be with anyone else but me" is a disrespectful judgment because you are telling your spouse how he or she feels. Truth is you don't know how your spouse feels, unless he or she tells you.

"I become upset when I'm left alone at night" is an honest feeling, because you are telling your spouse how *you* feel.

"If you don't start spending more time with me soon, I'll find someone else to spend time with" is a selfish demand.

"I'd like to spend more time with you" is an honest feeling.

In conquering the Love Buster of dishonesty, you must do more than just let out your feelings. You must make sure you express your feelings to your spouse in a way that informs without needlessly causing harm.

Honesty Helps You Aim at the Right Target

Most couples do their best to make each other happy—but their efforts, however sincere, are often misdirected. They aim at the wrong target.

Imagine a man who buys his wife flowers every night on the way home from work. What a wonderful thing to do—except his wife is allergic to them. Because she appreciates the gesture, she never mentions her allergies but just sniffles in silence. Soon, however, she begins to dread the thought of her husband coming home with those terrible flowers. Meanwhile, he's getting bored with the marriage because she is always feeling lousy and never has energy to do anything—because of her allergies. But of course he won't tell her that.

Their marriage is in trouble, not because of any lack of effort, but because of their ignorance—ignorance caused by dishonesty. He thinks he's doing a good thing by bringing home flowers but he doesn't realize that's the cause of their malaise. Let's say that, in his effort to show even more love for her, he brings home more and more flowers. Ultimately she's collapsed on the couch, gasping for breath, surrounded by flowers, while he wonders what went wrong.

It's a preposterous story but it portrays the way many couples misfire in their attempts to please each other. Their lack of honesty keeps them from correcting their real problems. To protect each other or to avoid trouble, husbands and wives often misinform each other about their feelings, activities, and plans. This not only leads to a withdrawal of love units when the deception is discovered, it also makes marital conflicts impossible to resolve. As conflicts build, romantic love slips away.

How Honest Should We Be?

You may agree with me that spouses should be honest with each other but you may wonder how far honesty should go. For couples

I counsel, I have written a rule to describe the depth of honesty I want them to experience. I call it the Rule of Honesty for Successful Marriage.

The Rule of Honesty for Successful Marriage

Reveal to your spouse as much information about yourself as you know: your thoughts, feelings, habits, likes, dislikes, personal history, daily activities, and plans for the future.

To help explain this rule, I have broken it down into five parts:

1. *Emotional Honesty:* Reveal your emotional reactions—both positive and negative—to the events of your life, particularly to your spouse's behavior.
2. *Historical Honesty:* Reveal information about your personal history, particularly events that demonstrate personal weakness or failure.
3. *Current Honesty:* Reveal information about the events of your day. Provide your spouse with a calendar of your activities, with special emphasis on those that may affect your spouse.
4. *Future Honesty:* Reveal your thoughts and plans regarding future activities and objectives.
5. *Complete Honesty:* Do not leave your spouse with a false impression about your thoughts, feelings, habits, likes, dislikes, personal history, daily activities, or plans for the future. Do not deliberately keep personal information from your spouse.

To some extent this rule seems like motherhood and apple pie. Who would argue that it's *not* a good idea to be honest? But in my years of experience as a marriage counselor, I have regularly struggled with the belief of many clients that dishonesty can be a good idea under certain conditions. Moreover, even some pastors and counselors advise dishonesty on occasion.

To those who argue that dishonesty can be justified under certain circumstances, I must say that my rule of honesty leaves no room for exceptions.

But because there are so many out there who *advocate* dishonesty in marriage, I need to build a case for my position. Let's take a careful look at each of the five parts of this rule, beginning with emotional honesty.

Emotional Honesty

> Reveal your emotional reactions—both positive and negative—to the events of your life, particularly to your spouse's behavior.

Some people find it difficult to express their emotional reactions, particularly the negative ones. They may fear that others will judge them for their feelings or they may be judging themselves, telling themselves they should not feel the way they do. They may doubt their ability to express negative feelings without demands, judgments, or anger. Or, wanting unconditional acceptance from their spouse, they may think their negative reactions prove their own inability to be unconditionally accepting.

But negative feelings serve a valuable purpose in a marriage. They are a signal that something is wrong. If you successfully steer clear of angry outbursts, disrespectful judgments, and selfish demands, your expression of negative feelings can alert both you and your spouse to an adjustment that must be made.

Honesty enables a couple to make appropriate adjustments to each other. Adjustment is what a good marriage is all about. The circumstances that led you into your blissful union will certainly change, if they haven't already, and you need to learn to roll with the tide. Both of you are growing and changing with each new day and you must constantly adjust to each other's changes. But how can you know how to adjust if you're not receiving accurate information about these changes? You'd be flying blind, like a pilot whose instrument panel has shorted out.

You need accurate data from each other. Without this, unhappy situations can go on and on—like the flowers piling up in the allergic woman's home. But if you communicate your feelings to each other, you can correct what you're doing wrong before it becomes a habit.

If Jennifer had told Ed how his behavior was affecting her on their honeymoon, for instance, he could have made an adjustment to accommodate her. If he had told her he was becoming dissatisfied with their sexual relationship, she could have adjusted for him. Instead, their dissatisfaction continued and grew, putting their marriage in jeopardy.

The mere communication of feelings does not assure that all the necessary adjustments will be made. There is still work to do. But without honest communication, failure is *guaranteed*.

Communication, of course, is a two-way street. Honest feelings need to be expressed *and received*. Complaints must be heard and honored. If you're getting the data, you must read it. The fact is both Jennifer and Ed *did* mention their frustration—on rare occasions. But because neither immediately received a positive response, they abandoned further explanations.

This illustrates the importance of persistence. Your commitment to honesty does not end when you have reported a feeling. A couple must continue to express feelings honestly to each other until the problem is resolved.

In other words, for honesty to have taken place in this relationship, Jennifer should have regularly confronted her husband with her loneliness, because she was lonely regularly. He was responsible to hear her, understand her, and make appropriate adjustments, but Jennifer needed to keep her message beacon on until the danger had passed.

Ed should have done the same with his sexual frustration. Yes, Jennifer needed to pay more attention than she did, but Ed needed to present his feelings in a way that grabbed her attention, so they could work together to find a solution.

We've been discussing the difficulty and importance of expressing negative emotions but we should not overlook the expression of positive feelings. While these are generally easier to communicate, many couples have not learned to express positive feelings either. By this failure, they miss an important opportunity to *deposit* love units. Whenever your spouse makes *you* feel good, if you express those feelings clearly and enthusiastically, you'll make *your spouse* feel good, knowing that his or her care is appreciated.

Historical Honesty

> Reveal information about your personal history, particularly events that demonstrate personal weakness or failure.

Should your skeletons stay in the closet?

Some say yes: Lock the door, hide the key, leave well enough alone. Communicate your past misdeeds only on a need-to-know basis.

But I say your spouse always needs to know. Whatever embarrassing experiences or serious mistakes are in your past, you need to come clean with your spouse in the present.

Your personal history holds significant information about you, information about your strengths and weaknesses. For your spouse to make necessary adjustments to you, he or she needs to understand both your good and bad points. Where can you be relied on? Where do you need help?

For example, if a man has had an affair in the past, he may be vulnerable to another one. If a woman has been chemically dependent in the past, she'll be susceptible to drug or alcohol abuse in the future. If you express your past mistakes openly, your spouse can understand your weaknesses, and together you can avoid conditions that tend to create problems for you.

No area of your life should be kept secret. All questions asked by your spouse should be answered fully and completely. Periods of poor adjustment in your past should be given special attention. Those previous conditions should be carefully understood, since problems of the past are commonly problems of the future.

Not only should *you* explain your past to your spouse, but you should encourage your spouse to gather information from *those who knew you* before you met. I encourage couples who are considering marriage to talk with several significant people from each other's past. It's often an eye-opener!

I include in this Rule of Historical Honesty the disclosure of all premarital and extramarital sexual relations. A husband and a wife *must* confide in each other, regardless of the reaction.

"But if I tell my wife about all the bad things I've done, she'll never trust me again."

"If my husband finds out about my past, he'll be crushed. It will ruin his whole image of me."

I have heard these protests from various clients, all ashamed of things they have done. Why dig it all up? Let that old affair stay buried in ancient history! Why not just leave that little demon alone? I answer that it's not a little demon but an extremely important part of their personal story and it says something about their character.

But what if you haven't strayed since it happened? What if you've seen a pastor regularly to hold you accountable? Why put your spouse through the agony of a revelation that could ruin your relationship forever?

I'd say you don't give your spouse much credit! Honesty does not drive a spouse away—*dishonesty* does. People in general, and women in particular, want to know exactly what their spouses are thinking and feeling. When you hold something back, your spouse tries to guess what it is. If he or she is right, then you must continually lie to cover your tracks. If wrong, your spouse develops an incorrect under-standing of you and your predispositions.

Maybe you don't really want to be known for who you are. That's the saddest position of all to be in. You'd rather keep your secret than experience one of life's greatest joys—to be loved and accepted in spite of known weaknesses.

While revealing your past is a good thing to do, it's not always pain-less. Some spouses have difficulty adjusting to revelations that have been kept secret for years—the saints they thought they married turn out to be not so saintly. To control the emotional damage, you may want to make your revelations in the presence of a professional counselor. Some spouses with emotional weaknesses may need some personal counseling to help them adjust to the reality of their spouse's past.

In many cases the spouse reacts more negatively to the long-term deception than to the concealed event. The thoughtless act might be easily accepted and forgiven, but the cover-up is often harder to accept.

You may be daunted by the idea of revealing your past and that's understandable. But let me assure you that I've never seen a mar-riage destroyed by truth. When truth is revealed, there are often neg-ative reactions and some shaky times, but ultimately the truth makes marriages stronger. On the other hand, dishonesty destroys intimacy, romantic love, and marriages.

Current Honesty

> Reveal information about the events of your day. Provide your spouse with a calendar of your activities, with special emphasis on those that may affect your spouse.

After six years of being married to Jennifer, and being sexually frustrated for much of that time, Ed discovered a woman at the office named Peggy. She became a welcome solution to his sexual problems. He spent time alone with her several times a week and their sexual relationship was as fulfilling as he ever could have imagined.

How did Ed justify this infidelity? As he saw it, he was doing Jennifer a favor by not imposing himself on her sexually. Whenever Jennifer wanted to make love to him, he happily accommodated her, but she didn't feel a sexual need more than two or three times a month. It was easier for both of them, he figured, if he turned to Peggy the rest of the time.

But of course he couldn't tell that to Jennifer. He still loved her very much and he knew that news of his affair would upset her. So once again to protect her from emotional pain, he chose to follow a course of dishonesty. This meant that he had to keep quiet about his daily schedule. If Jennifer guessed that he was making time for Peggy, the whole arrangement would be ruined.

In good marriages couples become so interdependent that sharing a daily schedule is essential to their coordination of activities. But in weak marriages the partners are reluctant to reveal their schedules because they often engage in the "annoying activities" Love Buster. Assuming that their spouse would object to these activities, they hide the details of their day, telling themselves, *What he doesn't know won't hurt him* or *She's happier not knowing everything.*

Even when activities are innocent, it's extremely important for your spouse to understand what you do with your time. Make sure you're easy to find in an emergency or when your spouse just wants to say hello during the day. Give each other your daily schedule so you can communicate about how you spend your day. Almost everything you do will affect your spouse, so it's important to explain what you do.

If Jennifer and Ed had established a habit of exchanging daily information early in their marriage, his affair would have been almost impossible to arrange. In fact if they had practiced the Rule of Honesty, his problem probably would have been resolved years earlier.

Honesty is a terrific way to protect your spouse from potentially damaging activities. When you know that you'll be telling your spouse what you've been up to, you're far less likely to get into trouble.

Future Honesty

> Reveal your thoughts and plans regarding future activities and objectives.

After I've made such a big issue of revealing past indiscretions, you can imagine how I feel about revealing future plans. They're *much* easier to discuss with your spouse, yet many couples make plans independently of each other. Why?

Some people believe that communicating future plans just gives a spouse the opportunity to quash them. They have their sights set on a certain goal and they don't want anything to stand in their way. Others just think their spouse wouldn't be interested.

No matter how innocent your plans are, when you fail to tell your spouse about them, you're engaging in a Love Buster. You may be trying to avoid trouble in the present, but eventually the future will arrive and your plans will be revealed. At that point your spouse will be hurt that you didn't communicate what you were planning. And that will withdraw love units.

The Policy of Joint Agreement—*Never do anything without an enthusiastic agreement between you and your spouse*—is certainly relevant in discussions of your future plans.

"If I wait for my wife to agree," a husband might say, "we'll never accomplish anything. She's so conservative, she never wants to take any risks, and so we miss every opportunity that comes along." But isn't that approach, in essence, a disrespectful judgment, forcing the husband's opinion on the wife? If he genuinely respects her, he will want her input on the decision—and more than mere input, her enthusiastic agreement!

"Oh, but the plans I make are best for both of us," a wife might say. "He may not understand my decision now but once he sees how things turn out, he'll thank me for going ahead with it." But to make plans independently and conceal them from your spouse is still a Love Buster. Granted, you won't lose love units until later but you *will* lose them. Even if your plans work out, your spouse will still feel bad about not being included in the planning.

Complete Honesty

> Do not leave your spouse with a false impression about your thoughts, feelings, habits, likes, dislikes, personal history, daily activities, or plans for the future. Do not deliberately keep personal information from your spouse.

It goes without saying: False impressions are just as deceitful as outright lies! The purpose of honesty is having the facts in front of you. Without them, you'll fail to solve the simplest marital problems. Why should it make a difference how you fail to reveal the facts to each other, whether by lies or by giving false impressions? Either one will leave your spouse ignorant.

I need to ask probing questions during premarital counseling. Knowing the areas where people tend to leave false impressions, that's where I probe most deeply. Since most marital problems originate with serious misconceptions, I do what I can to dig out these little weeds that eventually choke the plant.

Chances are the biggest false impression you may be giving is that your spouse does a good job of meeting your needs. And your spouse is probably letting you believe that you're doing well at meeting his or her needs. The truth is that in some areas both of you are probably quite dissatisfied.

No one ever wants to be accused of failure, so you run the risk of withdrawing love units if you express your dissatisfaction. But, as we saw earlier, it isn't honesty itself that withdraws love units, but the situation revealed by honesty—that emotional needs are not being met. And you can minimize the loss of love units by expressing your concerns in nonthreatening, nonjudgmental ways.

Only the true expression of your feelings will help you find a solution to your problems. Deception, even in the form of false impressions, can only lead to continuing misery. You *cripple* your spouse when you fail to reveal the truth. You provide a map that leads nowhere.

Not Everyone Values Honesty

In counseling, Dan confessed to me that he had been unfaithful early in his marriage. Should he tell his wife, Amy, about something that happened twenty years ago? Images of lawsuits flashed before me. What if, after he told Amy, she left him—or killed him! What if she became so depressed she killed herself? Besides, Amy never had a clue about his affair and so he never had to lie to cover it up. Should Dan tell her something that would hurt her deeply even if she never asked him about it?

His question tested my commitment to honesty. I believe we should always be truthful, especially in marriage, and most people would generally agree. But should we reveal incriminating facts about ourselves that would never be known otherwise? Even in our court system, honesty does not reach that level—you are not required to incriminate yourself.

I gave Dan advice based on my belief that honesty is one of our most important moral objectives. I warned him of what might happen after he told her—she might become violently angry or severely depressed—but I felt it was more important for him to be honest than to avoid the consequences of honesty.

Easy for you to say, you may be thinking. *How could you "shame" a person into doing something that could have turned into a disaster for himself, his wife, or both of them? It's just not a responsible thing for a professional counselor to do!*

I had those very same thoughts at the time but I still felt that honesty was more important than its consequences, good or bad. If Dan was going to be completely honest with his wife, that twenty-year-old affair was standing in his way.

Dan called me at 11 P.M. that night in a panic. He had confessed the affair to Amy and asked her to forgive him. She was devastated. What should he do now?

"Stay with her," I said. "Talk about it as much as she wants to. Don't make excuses or raise any other defenses. Just apologize."

I must admit that I worried about the outcome of this situation. Would honesty prove to be the best policy, or would it tear Dan and Amy apart?

After Dan dropped his bombshell, he and Amy were up all night, hashing it out, with many tears and recriminations. When the turmoil finally ended, the revelation of Dan's affair had not ruined the marriage. It did just the opposite. It brought them closer together. Dan and Amy committed themselves to a marriage based on the Rule of Honesty and the Policy of Joint Agreement. They would never again allow dishonesty to come between them and they would not do anything without each other's enthusiastic agreement. Under those conditions, Amy could trust Dan more than ever.

Over the next few years, whenever I suggested honesty at all costs, I kept waiting for that first case where honesty would blow the marriage apart. It never came. In case after case, honesty was a healer of marriages, not a destroyer. What began as a purely moral choice for me became a practical one. Honesty works. Now, after recommending complete honesty to hundreds of couples, I can tell you this principle is a proven marriage saver.

It's still an unpopular idea. Most marriage counselors argue that it's cruel to disclose past sexual affairs. They believe that the only reason you would reveal past indiscretion is to get it off your chest. This hurts your spouse so much that the truly caring thing, according to these counselors, is to lie about it or at least keep it tucked away.

I'm still horrified whenever I hear such nonsense and I hear it quite often. While it's true that honesty releases a great burden of guilt, emotional relief is not the only reason to be honest. Honesty is the door to understanding and it's what each of us deserves from our spouse. It often causes some pain in the short term but it helps couples avoid serious mistakes that lead to much greater pain farther down the road. Honesty is essential to a marriage's safety and success.

If you've been unfaithful to your spouse, that's an extremely important thing for someone to know about you. In fact an affair is one of the most memorable events of your life, however upsetting or embarrassing it may be. But it is more than an important event; it is also evidence that you can't be trusted, and your spouse should know that about you.

Honesty is a form of protection. The more that people know about you, the better able they are to protect themselves from your destructive predispositions. If you want to protect your spouse, he or she needs to know about ways that you could cause harm. If your spouse knows about your weaknesses, you can both make adjustments so that your failure is less likely. On the other hand, if your spouse is ignorant of them, he or she will be left defenseless.

Are you afraid that your spouse will leave you if you divulge your past errors? Let's think about that for a moment. Does that mean that your marriage is held together by lies? Doesn't your spouse have the right to know the person he or she married? Yes, and your spouse has the right to leave you—but this is very unlikely. As painful as it is to find out about an affair, very few ever divorce because of it. In most cases, both spouses make adjustments that help avoid a repeat. But without the truth, there is little assurance that it will not happen again. And *that's* what breaks up marriages—ongoing or repeated affairs—not the honest, penitent confession of past affairs.

Most people have affairs because of unmet emotional needs. If your needs are not being met by your spouse, you will be tempted to be unfaithful again. You and your spouse need to work together to guarantee that (1) you are both meeting each other's emotional needs and (2) you will never have another affair. You may need to set rules for yourself that prevent you from developing friendships and spending time alone with anyone who could replace your spouse in meeting your unmet emotional needs. Sexual fulfillment is just one of our many important emotional needs, but these also include conversation, affection, recreational companionship, admiration, and others. Any of these, when not being primarily met by your spouse, can be the avenue into an affair. You need to spend most of your free time with your spouse—your best friend should be the one to whom you are married.

After you reveal your indiscretion, don't keep anything from your spouse again—be as honest with him or her as you can be. You'll find that honesty will not only help you create a very intimate relationship, but it will also help prevent you from hurting your spouse again.

In our society a major weapon against crime is the video camera. We see them in stores and banks, and now some towns are putting them outside, in public areas. The theory is this: We commit crimes more easily when we think people won't know about it. The cameras invade personal privacy to some extent but they keep people honest.

I've wondered about that theory in everyday life. If all our acts were videotaped for anyone to see, what effect would that have on our behavior? I suspect most of us would be more thoughtful and caring—and certainly more honest.

Self-imposed honesty is the next best thing to videotape. If you know that you will reveal to your spouse whatever you do, you are far less likely to do things that will hurt him or her. This essentially eliminates affairs. If you go one step farther and follow my Policy of Joint Agreement—*Never do anything without an enthusiastic agreement between you and your spouse*—affairs are utterly impossible.

Creating an Environment for Honesty

When you are on the receiving end of such honest disclosures, you should try to reward your spouse for honesty. Most people do the opposite. Finally presented with the truth about something that had been concealed, many spouses think only of punishment. They cry, they scream, they hit, they threaten—and all these things just convince the lying partner to cover his or her crimes more carefully in the future. Don't put your spouse through hell because he or she failed to tell you the truth. That would simply encourage dishonesty the next time. Instead, talk about how important honesty is to you and how you want to work together to achieve a more honest marriage. Use the disclosure as evidence that you both need to rise to a new level of honesty.

How well do you encourage honesty? You may say that you want your spouse to be honest, but do your own values promote it? Do your reactions convey an appreciation for the truth, even if it's painful? To see how you rate, answer these questions:

1. If the truth is terribly upsetting to you, do you want your spouse to be honest only at a time when you are emotionally prepared?
2. Do you keep some aspects of your life secret and do you encourage your spouse to respect your privacy in those areas?
3. Have you defined your boundaries and do you encourage your spouse not to cross them?
4. Do you like to create a certain mystery between you and your spouse?
5. Are there conditions under which you would not want honesty at all costs between you and your spouse?
6. Do you ever have angry outbursts when your spouse is honest with you?
7. Do you ever make disrespectful judgments when your spouse is honest with you?
8. Do you ever make selfish demands when your spouse is honest with you?

If you answer yes to any of the first five questions, you tend to compromise on honesty. Apparently you feel your marriage is better off with dishonesty in certain situations. That little crack is all dishonesty needs to slip into your marriage and run amok. You see, there are always "reasons" to be dishonest. As soon as you allow one, it begins to blur into all the rest, and before you know it, you have a dishonest relationship.

If you answered yes to questions 6, 7, or 8, you are inadvertently encouraging dishonesty. The way to help your spouse learn to be truthful is to minimize the negative consequences of his or her truthful revelations. Instead of trying to punish your spouse for thoughtless acts, emphasize a safe and pleasant negotiation, when he or she is free to work out alternatives that are genuinely attractive to both of you.

If your spouse is forced to agree with you just to survive, you invite dishonesty. Your spouse will learn to agree with anything to avoid a fight—and then do what he or she pleases. But what if there are no fights? No judgments? No demands? If you can eliminate these Love Busters, you'll make it much easier for your spouse to be honest with you.

In part 2, we'll discuss some of the most common conflicts in marriage. I'll show you how Love Busters have made these conflicts impossible to solve; then I'll show you how eliminating Love Busters and applying the Policy of Joint Agreement to the conflicts make their solutions possible.

Part 2

RESOLVING
MARITAL
CONFLICTS

Resolving Conflicts over Friends and Relatives 7

M any parents make the sad mistake of not letting go. But their habit of dictating their child's every move can be devastating to the child's marriage.

Shortly after the wedding, Sherrie told Dwight that to keep peace in her family he must join Trinity Church, where her parents attended. Having been a member of Saint Paul Community Church all his life, he preferred continuing to attend there. Besides, he and Sherrie had attended his church together before their wedding, and she loved it. But Sherrie insisted, so he agreed.

For about a year, Dwight attended Trinity with Sherrie but was never able to make the adjustment. He complained to her all year about how unfair it was that her parents decided what church they should attend.

One day he'd had it. "Sherrie, I just can't do it anymore. I will not attend a church just to make your parents happy."

"Well, then do it to make me happy."

"But I'm not comfortable at that church. Besides, you always enjoyed being at my church before we were married. What's so bad about it now?"

"Dwight, I enjoy the services at your church but I can't disappoint my parents."

"You *can't* disappoint your parents but you *can* disappoint me, right?"

When the couple saw me for counseling, I pointed out to Sherrie that she'd been making a selfish demand, gaining peace with her parents at the expense of her husband's feelings. She knew he did not enjoy the church services yet she forced him to attend so she would not have to deal with her parents' rejections.

Dwight had made the correct response to her demand: He rejected it. He told her he would not continue to do something that made him uncomfortable. They needed to find a solution that would satisfy them both, and his attending Trinity was not it.

The concept of selfish demands was like a breath of fresh air for Sherrie. She had struggled with the issue of whom to please, Dwight or her parents, ever since they'd married. Now she saw that whenever she tried to force Dwight to do something for her parents it was just as selfish as if it were for herself. I pointed out to her that in a sense it *was* for herself.

She felt as if she'd had a heavy burden lifted from her shoulders. They had already attended several other churches and discussed these alternatives. None of them would have pleased her parents, but with their new perspective they moved beyond that problem. Now they were simply looking for a church they would both enjoy.

After lengthy discussions, they agreed that they enjoyed and benefited most from the services at Saint Paul Community and should return to that church. Sherrie was very happy with the outcome.

When told of their decision, Sherrie's parents announced that they would not speak to Sherrie and Dwight until they changed their minds. Sherrie had experienced this reaction in the past, because her family was into demands and intimidation. But this time she didn't buckle under the pressure. She and Dwight decided to honor her parents' request for silence. It took two full years, but her parents finally broke the silence and admitted they'd made a mistake.

Dwight and Sherrie's solution to the problem met the conditions of the Policy of Joint Agreement. They both rejected other solutions until they had each other's enthusiastic support for one. Their final solution deposited love units into both Love Banks and protected their romantic love.

In the end, Sherrie's parents adjusted to their decision. But even if they had not, the decision would have been correct. As their counselor, I witnessed a noticeable improvement in the love Dwight and Sherrie felt for each other, and their entire family benefited.

Taking Generosity One Step Too Far

Judy had always been generous. That's one of the traits that attracted Bill to her. But after their marriage he began to feel drained by her generosity. She had never earned much money, and he had. That's one of the traits that attracted her to him!

"We can't support your sister and brother-in-law, Judy. He'll have to find a job, just like everyone else."

"But he tried, and if we don't help, who will? Please, Bill," she begged, "let's help them just one more time."

They did help. But it wasn't just that time; it was many times thereafter. Eventually Judy's sister and brother-in-law moved into Judy and Bill's house—and remained for five years. Both couples had a child during that time, which put an even greater strain on the situation.

When is it wrong to be generous? It's when you impose the cost of your generosity on someone else. It would have been one thing for both Judy and Bill to have agreed to be generous, but it was quite another for Judy to be generous at Bill's expense.

Judy enjoyed giving to her sister, so she did it whenever she had an opportunity. But as soon as Bill found out, he became furious. They had trouble paying their own bills, and when Judy gave away his monthly earnings, she put Bill under needless financial pressure. Her habit of generosity annoyed him. It was a Love Buster.

When Judy insisted on inviting her sister and brother-in-law to live with them, she made a selfish demand. Bill came home one day to find them ready to move in. Judy didn't ask if it was okay with him or give him a choice. It was a terrible invasion of their privacy, and they would have extreme difficulty arranging any time to be alone.

Again and again Bill tried to convince Judy that her relatives should leave, but she remained resolute. "I can't do that to my sister. You'll have to understand."

Bill may have tried to understand, but Judy's love units in his Love Bank kept drifting away until there were none left to withdraw. At that point, he could no longer tolerate the situation. Even though it meant leaving his child, whom he loved dearly, he felt he had to go.

Bill's decision brought them to me for counseling. I persuaded Judy to consider the effect of her generosity on her family. First she came to realize that her own child suffered. Then, and more important, she acknowledged that Bill had suffered from her generosity. She had been generous with Bill's money and effort but she had not been generous toward Bill.

The tenacity of Judy's effort to keep her sister's family at home with her amazed me. Even though Bill had moved out, she made every effort to resolve the conflict in a way that would keep her sister with her. As the counseling continued, Judy became more obviously selfish. She wanted her sister to be with her at all costs. Her handouts made her sister dependent on her, and that's how she wanted it.

Judy could see the wisdom of making joint decisions with Bill but had a very difficult time doing it. In the end, the realization that Bill would not put up with her Love Busters saved the day. She eventually chose to take Bill's feelings into account, because he would not come back if she did not.

She decided to become thoughtful and in the process created the conditions for Bill's love to return. Eventually her thoughtfulness toward him became firmly established, and they shared romantic love for each other.

Judy continued to be generous, but not at Bill's expense. She discussed each generous act with him and waited for his enthusiastic support before she went ahead with it.

I've counseled many individuals who complain of severe depression. After I've had an opportunity to get to know them, I often find that they've been forced by their spouse to endure an unpleasant lifestyle. In an effort to please their loved one, they agree to unbearable circumstances that eventually lead to depression. Once the unpleasant lifestyle is changed, their depression lifts.

My emphasis on the word *enthusiastic* in the Policy of Joint Agreement helps eliminate solutions to problems that might lead to depression. Remember, only enthusiastic support for a solution deposits love units. Certain personality types willingly endure pain in an effort to please others. They are willing to do things for others that can actually cause a withdrawal of love units from their Love Bank. If you're married to one of these individuals, don't let your husband or wife sacrifice responses to his or her own needs. Wait for enthusiastic support before you carry out your plan, or your spouse's romantic love for you will be at risk.

The Former Lover

When Sue asked Jack, her new husband, to have dinner with Sam, her former lover, Jack was dumbfounded.

"Have dinner with Sam? Are you crazy? He's the last person in the world I'd ever want to see," Jack complained.

But Sue's persistence paid off—for her. Jack reluctantly agreed to dine with Sam and Sue. She simply wanted to maintain a friendship with Sam and didn't want it to be behind Jack's back. That made sense to her.

Sue felt that Jack would eventually adjust to her friendship with Sam. But as you might expect, he didn't. Jack's memory of her selfish demand became the single most damaging event of their marriage. He never did get over it. But that's not where it ended.

Over the years, Sue continued to see Sam from time to time and she always told Jack about it. He always became upset when she told him, but it wasn't the honesty that withdrew love units, it was her persistence in an annoying activity.

It seems obvious to me that a former lover wouldn't be welcome in a marriage. But I guess if it were *my* former lover, it wouldn't be so obvious to me. What should have been obvious was that Sue enjoyed her friendship with Sam at Jack's expense. It was a Love Buster and it violated the Policy of Joint Agreement. Sue felt she had the right to see whomever she pleased. Marriage, she believed, should not restrain her basic personal freedoms.

Her indulgence in activities that benefited her at Jack's emotional expense eventually took its toll on him. Jack gradually lost his feeling of romantic love for Sue. When that happened, he began to engage in disrespectful judgments by being critical and rude. Of course, that withdrew love units from her Love Bank, and by the time they came to see me, they hated each other.

In my counseling, I first encouraged Jack to eliminate his critical and rude behavior. It was out of character for him to be that way, and he followed my recommendation without much difficulty.

Then Sue came to understand how her "freedom" had hurt Jack. She eventually apologized for what she had put Jack through and stopped seeing Sam.

The recovery of their romantic love was a long and difficult process, one they could have avoided if they had protected each other from Love Busters when they were first married. Their ability to meet each other's emotional needs had never been a problem, but their destructive habits prevented them from doing it. Once those habits were eliminated, slowly but surely they allowed each other to meet their emotional needs and restore their Love Bank balances.

Now they both understand and apply the Policy of Joint Agreement. Each time they have a conflict, they wait until they can both express enthusiasm for the solution. With each solution, they build romantic love.

"I Just Don't Like Her!"

Craig and Joan could not figure out how to resolve their problem. Craig knew there was really nothing wrong with Joan's friend, Bev, but she annoyed him. In fact he felt annoyed whenever Joan talked to Bev on the telephone. Craig believed Joan should be able to freely choose her friends, and she had known Bev long before she met him. He didn't want to break up that friendship but he just didn't like Bev, and Joan's relationship with her was beginning to affect their marriage.

They came to me for counseling and I helped them recognize that Joan's friendship with Bev was an annoying activity. It was innocent, as most annoying activities are, but it was a Love Buster. Each time Joan saw Bev, love units were withdrawn from Craig's Love Bank. The friendship was not worth the risk of losing romantic love.

Craig had no choice in the matter. His emotional reactions to Bev were strongly negative and consistent. He tried to like Bev, but it didn't work. Compromises had been attempted, but to no avail. In the end, it became apparent that Bev had to go.

Every one of us knows someone whom we dislike. I can't believe that Will Rogers wasn't annoyed by *someone!* It's normal to like some people and dislike others. Furthermore, just because you love your spouse there's no guarantee you'll like your spouse's friends.

Most of us who are married notice that the friends we had before marriage are not the same as those after marriage. Look at your wedding pictures. How many of those people do you still regard as close friends? For most of us, only those who were friends of *both* spouses before marriage remain friends after marriage.

Friendships are more difficult to develop than most people think. And they depend on individual taste. In general, there is nothing wrong with people I don't like, and there is nothing wonderful about people I do like. It seems that I'm programmed for certain people and not for others. Most people find this true.

After I convinced Joan that she needed to choose friends they both liked, she eventually eased out of her relationship with Bev. They have since formed new friendships, and Joan is just as happy with her new friends as she was with Bev. And her new friendships help her deposit love units in Craig's Love Bank.

"You Like Her Too Much"

Sometimes a problem develops in marriage when you like your spouse's friend *too* much. When you find yourself infatuated with a mutual friend, you're headed for deep trouble.

Tom and his wife, Alice, bought a mobile home in a resort community when they retired. They liked the area so much they encouraged their best friends, George and Emma, to buy the home for sale next door to them. It turned out to be a great idea, until George died.

After his death, the three of them remained very good friends. Tom was more than willing to help Emma with repairs and he often went over just to keep her company. Within a few months he had fallen in love with her. He didn't tell Alice about it but he did tell Emma. She was also in love with him. Before long he was doing more than keeping her company!

This went on for more than a year before Alice caught them. They were both ashamed and begged her forgiveness, but she could not be consoled. She didn't know what to do. Should she forgive her friend's offenses and continue the friendship? Or should she abandon the relationship forever?

This problem affects married couples of all ages. It is particularly troublesome among retired couples who have been lifelong friends. I know of more than twenty cases where the offending spouse was over seventy years of age. It's remarkable, yet predictable. Why *wouldn't* you fall in love with a lifelong friend?

Tom made his first mistake when he failed to tell Alice he was falling in love with Emma. If he had avoided the Love Buster dishonesty, the problem might have been nipped in the bud. Many affairs in the making can be safely sidetracked with honesty.

Tom had a million excuses why he kept the truth from Alice: He didn't want to hurt her feelings; he knew how important Emma's friendship was to Alice; it was a short-term fling that would end soon with no one the wiser.

Dishonesty always has its reasons. But it always brings the same result—solutions to marital problems become impossible because information critical to a solution is distorted.

Tom's second mistake was that he developed an annoying activity. His relationship with Emma was good for him but bad for Alice. He gained pleasure at her expense. His "activity," the affair, inflicted unbearable pain on Alice, once it was uncovered. He did not protect her from his own selfish behavior.

When they came to see me for counseling, I first taught Tom the importance of honesty. Over the next few weeks, he told Alice the details of the affair. She was terribly upset by his revelations but she recovered. He promised her he would never lie to her about anything again, even if it might hurt her feelings.

We then designed a plan to break Tom's habit of seeing Emma. I recommended they sell their mobile home and move to another retirement community in another state. Years of experience have taught me that people cannot be trusted with former lovers, and the close proximity to Emma would have been extremely hard on Alice.

The move was difficult but it prevented him from yielding to the occasional temptation to see Emma, and it kept Alice from worrying about their seeing each other behind her back.

Tom was willing to make the move, even though he still loved Emma. He believed he could be trusted and thought the move was unnecessary but he agreed because he wanted to put Alice's mind at ease.

Tom and Alice eventually restored romance to their marriage, and while it was a painful process, the positive outcome was something neither of them believed was possible. They had narrowly escaped marital and emotional disaster.

Many conflicts regarding friends and relatives pit the interests of a spouse against those of the friends and relatives. Your spouse is your most important friend and relative. No other should ever come between you.

Resolving Conflicts over   8
Career Choices

Moving is never easy but it's excruciatingly painful when you don't *want* to move. Jean was in tears all day as she packed.

"Brian, Duluth may be a wonderful city with wonderful opportunities, but I like it here in Sioux Falls. Please, don't do this to me," she begged.

"I'm sorry," he replied, shaking his head, "but we can't turn back now. I was fortunate to be offered this job and I can't pass it up."

Jean moved to Duluth with Brian. Then she moved to Des Moines, Kansas City, and finally Minneapolis. Their children had not been in one school for any two-year period and they were having trouble adjusting socially. Jean had experienced severe symptoms of anxiety, so she made an appointment with me to help her and her children.

During my first interview with her, she avoided the subject of her marriage and focused on her symptoms. But eventually she mentioned that her anxiety had threatened her marriage. Sometimes it's difficult to know if emotional symptoms cause a bad marriage or vice versa. I tentatively concluded it was probably the marriage that caused the symptoms and asked to see her husband.

Brian loved her dearly, tried to put her first in everything, valued his time with his family, and was intelligent and attractive besides. He seemed to be a perfect husband. But in my interview with him, he mentioned that Jean had been cold toward him ever since they moved from Sioux Falls. In further conversations with Jean, she admitted that the move had caused a change in her feelings toward Brian and she wasn't sure she loved him anymore. During the past year, they had made love infrequently.

The more we talked about Sioux Falls, the more visibly depressed Jean became, mentioning on several occasions having no hope of ever going back "home."

I explained to Brian that his wife could take drugs to relieve the anxiety symptoms that seemed to be caused by all their moving around, or he could move the family back to Sioux Falls. If they moved, I predicted that within two to five years, she'd be back to normal. Even if I was wrong, it was worth a try. She was becoming increasingly neurotic and soon her treatment would become prohibitively expensive and painful for the whole family.

Brian was able to get an excellent job in Sioux Falls. The last I heard, Jean's love had been restored, she was no longer in therapy, and her anxiety symptoms had all but disappeared.

This case illustrates a major point: *You* usually know what you need better than anyone else. Jean knew she would suffer if she moved away from Sioux Falls. And she did suffer. But short of a divorce, she thought there was no way to return.

She experienced a conflict that commonly causes severe emotional symptoms: If she were to choose moving from one strange community to the next, she would suffer; and if she were to choose a divorce, she would suffer. This type of conflict is called an avoidance-avoidance conflict. In other words, it makes no difference what you do, you will experience pain. Conflicts like this tend to make people neurotic. In some cases, these conflicts lead to suicide.

Brian's insistence that the family move from one city to another was a selfish demand. If he had formulated his desire to move from Sioux Falls as a thoughtful request, they would not have moved, and none of this pain would have resulted. His mistake cost Jean years of unhappiness and caused his account in her Love Bank to become bankrupt.

When he finally withdrew his selfish demand and they returned to Sioux Falls, two things happened at the same time. First, Jean felt much better back home in Sioux Falls and eventually overcame her emotional disorder; second, the depletion of love units ended, and Brian began to rebuild his Love Bank account. Jean's romantic love for him was eventually restored.

My wife, Joyce, and I experienced a similar situation, but we handled it differently at the outset. I was offered an attractive career opportunity in Chicago, but Joyce was not at all happy about moving from beautiful Santa Barbara. After discussing alternatives, we came to an agreement: She was willing to go to Chicago on the condition that we would move back if she found that she preferred living in Santa Barbara.

After a year in Chicago, I was offered another opportunity in Minneapolis. Again, we discussed the alternatives, and Joyce agreed to the move as long as a return to Santa Barbara was possible.

During that year, my daughter, Jennifer, was placed in four different schools, and Joyce's father died suddenly and unexpectedly. It was a time of unprecedented emotional upheaval. But through it all Joyce knew I'd be willing to return to Santa Barbara as soon as she said the word.

There were disadvantages to be sure, but there were also advantages to living in Minneapolis. Joyce was able to weigh them in her mind and each year chose to remain in the Twin Cities. To this day she has never expressed a bit of resentment toward me regarding the move, because it was a *joint* decision. (As it turned out, she loves the Twin Cities, and she has been very happy living here.)

Is He Ambitious or a Workaholic?

Renee didn't know exactly what she wanted in a husband, but she knew one thing: She didn't want to marry a lazy oaf! So when Jim came along, his tireless ability to work impressed her. He had not only put himself through college but had saved enough to pay cash for his car. It made her feel secure to know he was not the type to pile up debts.

While they were dating, he saw her or at least called her every day. Being with her was a part of his schedule. But after they married, his career took off, and his time with Renee gradually lessened.

"Jim, you're working too hard," she would tell him. "Why don't you relax a little? Let's take a vacation together!"

He would just smile. "I am relaxed! Have you ever seen me on a vacation? I'm a bundle of nerves."

Jim didn't realize—and Renee didn't explain—that the problem was not his nerves but their relationship. They were not with each other often enough to sustain romance. They couldn't possibly meet each other's emotional needs, and Renee had become very lonely.

Renee came to me to express her dissatisfaction with life. She lived in a beautiful home and had wonderful children and all the freedom a mother could ever dream of. But she lacked romance. In fact she was seriously considering an affair, just to see if it would help.

She had indulged in the Love Buster dishonesty by failing to explain to Jim that she was unhappy with their relationship. She didn't want to appear unappreciative of all the material things he provided. And she didn't dare tell him she was thinking of having an affair. He might leave her, and then where would she be?

Arranging for an appointment with Jim was a Herculean task. He was scheduled for months ahead. I adjusted my schedule to fit his. Even then, he canceled at the last minute when a "business emergency" arose.

When I finally did see him, I asked if he felt his schedule was any of Renee's business.

He was puzzled by my question. "Of course it's her business," he responded.

Then I wanted to know if he had ever asked her how she felt about his schedule. He thought he had, but Renee was right there to tell him he hadn't.

Finally, I asked him if Renee's feelings would affect his schedule. If she was unhappy with something he planned, would he change his plans to accommodate her feelings?

By the end of the session, Jim had gotten the message. His work schedule had become his highest priority, and even though he said he was working to make Renee happy, he was actually doing it to make himself happy. He had imposed his work schedule on Renee, and his career fulfillment came at her expense.

They did not spend enough time with each other to meet their most important emotional needs. If Renee had expressed satisfaction with that arrangement, I would have concluded that she was in the withdrawal stage. She would have wanted him gone so she wouldn't suffer from his inattentiveness. But, thankfully, she wasn't satisfied with his absence. She still wanted to be with him.

Over the next few weeks, Jim cooperated with Renee in creating a new schedule. It didn't include the thoughtless activities that peppered his old schedule. Instead, each event on his calendar met with her approval, and his career no longer withdrew love units from her Love Bank.

They fulfilled one of my counseling objectives, which was to set aside fifteen hours each week to give each other undivided attention (*see* chapter 13). During those hours Jim was able to meet Renee's most important emotional needs, depositing much-needed love units in the process.

In the final analysis, Jim was still a workaholic in the sense that he enjoyed work more than most people do. But when Jim gave Renee's feelings a higher priority than his career, he saved his marriage and possibly his career as well.

Renee's habit of dishonesty was part of their problem. Jim had always been willing to accommodate her feelings, but she needed to express them before he could make an adjustment.

I've counseled others, however, who were not as accommodating as Jim. They argue that unless they devote all their energy and effort to their career, their family will become homeless! These people have their priorities backward.

Your career should serve your marriage, your marriage should not serve your career. You and your spouse should work with each other to help develop each other's career, but the success of your careers should never be more important to you than the success of your marriage. To put it another way, the success of your career should never be at the expense of your spouse's feelings.

I've spoken to many people who are close to death, and none of them have ever told me they should have spent more time at work. If people have regrets later in life, it's that they didn't spend more time with their spouse and children.

Flying into Clouds of Conflict

Any career that takes you away from your spouse overnight is dangerous to the health of your marriage. The more you're gone, the more dangerous it is.

I can thank the airline industry for giving me the opportunity to make a living as a marriage counselor. Their employees helped me become an expert on the subject of infidelity, because many of these folks were having affairs in almost every way possible. They also gave me confidence in my methods, since these couples provided such a difficult testing ground, and the methods proved successful even under those conditions.

Sarah absolutely loved her job as a flight attendant. She liked the work itself, earned a good salary, and could travel almost anywhere as an employee benefit. Her husband, Rich, didn't like her job at all. She had applied for it without consulting him, knowing he wouldn't like the idea and thinking she probably wouldn't get it anyway. But when they actually offered it to her, she was delirious with excitement.

When Rich came in the door from work, Sarah flung her arms around his neck. "I got it! I got it!"

He smiled and hugged her back. "Got what?"

"I got a job as a flight attendant. Isn't that great? Oh, I'm so happy!"

Rich's smile faded. But Sarah didn't notice. She ran all around their apartment, screaming, "I got it!"

"Hey, wait a minute, Sarah, you didn't tell me you were applying for a new job. Don't you like the one you already have?"

"It was okay, but I never thought I'd be able to work as a flight attendant. It's all right with you, isn't it?"

Rich didn't seem to have a choice. "Well, I guess we can try it for a while to see how it works but I'm not too crazy about your being away so much."

Six months later the job was becoming a major issue in their marriage. Rich was not only being left alone for up to three nights at a time, but he was becoming jealous of the pilots and passengers who asked his wife out to dinner. Sarah would come home to find a beast in her apartment, and by the time he'd settle down, she'd be off on another trip.

When they came for counseling, Sarah was not sure she was in love with Rich anymore because he had become so abusive. She thought she might be falling in love with someone she met on a flight. A separation might be a good idea, she suggested, so she could decide how she felt about her marriage.

Rich didn't know about any of this and simply wanted me to tell her to quit her job.

The marriage hung together by a thread. Even though she engaged in the Love Buster annoying activities, it would have been foolish to tell her to stop. I would not only have been making a demand, which I don't believe in doing, but she probably wouldn't have shown up for the next appointment.

So I had to begin therapy with Rich. He was guilty of angry outbursts, disrespectful judgments, and selfish demands. While it's true that they were in response to the pain he felt over Sarah's job, they had not resolved the problem and had caused Sarah to lose romantic love for him.

I explained that he would need to learn to control his abusive behavior before we could work on her annoying behavior. It was in *his* best interests to control his temper and stop making demands. In return for his commitment to avoid these Love Busters, she agreed not to separate while in counseling.

His success in avoiding angry outbursts was probably the most crucial step toward their recovery. Once she felt he could control his temper, she could explain her feelings to him and even went so far as to tell him that she had been planning to move out, that she might be in love with someone else, and that she didn't love him.

Even then he didn't lose his temper. He simply expressed his desire for reconciliation.

At that point in the counseling process, I had the opportunity to explain to her that she'd been inconsiderate of his feelings when she took her job. She had gained a career advantage at his expense.

Her face turned red. "Well, I suppose you want me to quit my job. That's what you really want, isn't it?"

I explained that she could do anything she wanted. I had no right to demand anything of her, and neither did Rich. But the truth was that her happiness led to his pain.

They began a process of negotiation that followed my Policy of Joint Agreement. After they agreed that neither of them should gain at each other's expense, Sarah found another job with the same airline company, one Rich enthusiastically supported because it gave her many of the same benefits yet didn't require being away nights.

The happy ending did not take place overnight. Many times I thought the process might end in failure. But the intelligence of the process won out over the foolishness of the alternatives. Sarah had lost romantic love, but I kept assuring her that it could be regained if Rich continued his thoughtfulness. His efforts clearly saved the day, and once her feelings toward him improved, she was more willing to be thoughtful herself.

What If God's Calling Is the Issue?

I'll repeat what I said earlier: Your career should serve your marriage; your marriage should not serve your career. Those who use their marriage to serve career, often lose the marriage. This can even happen to those motivated by a desire to serve God.

When he was nine, Al committed his life to the ministry. At a church service, when the preacher asked for a commitment from those willing to become full-time ministers, he responded and never forgot that decision. In college he majored in Bible to prepare for the ministry.

Toni was also a Bible major and had thought of becoming a missionary. They took many of the same classes and studied together. They dated and before long they were in love.

Before graduation Toni decided against becoming a missionary, changed her major to social work, and eventually completed that major. Al figured social work would be a great background for a minister's wife and encouraged her in her professional training.

They married immediately after college graduation. He enrolled in seminary, and she found a job as a social worker. After one year of seminary, they both realized Toni was not comfortable in the role of a minister's wife.

"Toni, we're in this thing together. You have an important role to play," Al explained. When she expressed reluctance to accept that role, he trotted out Bible verses on the subject of a man's authority over his wife.

Toni became furious. "Don't you lecture me. I'll do what I please and if I don't want to play Mrs. Reverend, I won't."

Then they broke into the biggest fight they'd ever had. When it was over, Toni agreed to support him in his ministry but she didn't like it at all. It certainly wasn't "enthusiastic agreement."

Al had made disrespectful judgments and selfish demands that would eventually come back to haunt him.

After graduating from seminary, Al took a position in a rural church of fifty members. He was happy with his career, but Toni suffered. She could not fit the role expected of her. There was little privacy in the church parsonage, and she hated living in a fishbowl. She put on a cheerful face when she met parishioners but when she was home alone, she cried.

Al felt her problems were spiritual and that she had not given herself to God's work. Her "rebellious spirit" was keeping her from enjoying the ministry as much as he enjoyed it. She believed him and her depression became so bad that she could no longer hide it from others, and eventually Al felt she should see a psychologist.

It didn't take me long to discover the problem. She explained that she was not cut out for the role of pastor's wife. What's worse, she had come to hate her husband, a feeling she'd never felt toward anyone before. Because she couldn't tolerate the feeling of hatred toward anyone, she was on the brink of suicide. She thought she might be possessed.

Al had imposed his career on Toni, even though he knew she suffered as a result. He also demanded that she perform duties to further his ministry, even though they were painful to her.

The solution to their problem started with eliminating the mistakes that created it. I convinced Al that disrespectful judgments were not at all helpful. Pastors are in the habit of making moral judgments from the pulpit and often carry their preaching into their home. Al was no exception, and Toni had become a captive audience. He had to learn to talk to her without any reference to "shoulds" and "oughts."

He also came to understand the destructiveness of his selfish demands. He learned not to try to force her into any particular role in the church, hoping that she would eventually find a comfortable way to help him.

Unfortunately, Toni had developed such an aversion to the entire scene that they both eventually came to the conclusion that he needed to make a career change to accommodate her.

As they discussed alternatives with each other, they settled on a career in counseling as mutually acceptable. Toni was able to find a full-time job as a social worker, which supported his retraining. The work was good for her, and I saw them long enough to see her recover from depression.

He has now completed his retraining, has a job as a psychologist, and last I heard Toni was in love with him again. He works closely with churches and supports ministers in their pastoral counseling.

It's all a matter of priorities. In Al's case, he had to realize that once he was married, *Toni had to be his highest priority.* His marriage could not serve his career. His career had to serve his marriage, even though his career was the Christian ministry.

He did not have to make a choice between God and Toni. Al believed he had made his commitments to both his career and his wife as God directed. The question was, *Which is more important to God?* I firmly believe that his commitment to his wife was more important.

I've counseled many pastors and their wives. In many cases, the men made a commitment to become a minister of the gospel long before they met their wife and their wife knew the seriousness of their commitment at the time of marriage.

However, in the course of life, these men discovered that they'd married women who, for whatever reason, had failed to adjust to the role of pastor's wife. At that point each had a decision to make: *Does God want me to follow my commitment to Christian ministry and remain a pastor, or do I reevaluate that commitment in light of the needs of my spouse?*

In some cases the man has no choice. His wife may have already left him, and if they're divorced he may not be able to continue in the ministry.

Those who still think they have a choice struggle with the decision. They think God will be disappointed with them if they choose to consider their wife's feelings in making career decisions. I point out to them how silly that sounds. How could God be disappointed with thoughtfulness toward their spouse? He's in *favor* of thoughtfulness, not *opposed* to it!

The solution is found in the Policy of Joint Agreement. When a wife realizes her husband is willing to negotiate a new career with her, she will usually take her husband's love for the ministry into account. The decision often keeps them in the ministry, but provides an emotionally satisfying role for the wife.

I planned my career with my wife in mind. My first career choice was to become a minister, my second was medicine, and my third was law enforcement. Joyce didn't like any of them for various reasons.

By the time we had been married three years, we both agreed on the profession I have now, psychology. As an undergraduate, I had not taken even an introductory course in psychology, and my graduate school training in psychology had to begin with the fundamentals.

It would have been pointless to start my career development without her support. After all, my career was to be a joint effort with joint compensation. If at some time she had second thoughts about the way it was turning out, I was prepared to abandon psychology to take up a new profession. Without her support, the career would not serve our mutual purposes in life. Her encouragement has made my choice particularly satisfying and undoubtedly accounts for much of its success.

Joyce's career choices were made with the same consideration for my feelings. I support her career as enthusiastically as she supports mine. I consider her work as a gospel singer and radio host/producer to be an effort we make jointly. I never resent the time she spends pursuing her career interests, because she is willing to accommodate my feelings with her schedule and choice of career activities.

Since we are both ambitious people, our career interests could have wrecked our marriage. But instead, our careers have strengthened our marriage, because we consider each other more important than our work.

Resolving Conflicts over Financial Planning 9

Frank didn't seem to worry about his finances. He earned enough to get by, and that was always good enough for him. But he never borrowed money.

After high school, he had moved from his home into a mortuary where he worked (while he slept) as night attendant. He earned free meals at his part-time job as waiter and took the bus whenever he needed transportation. Grants paid part of his college expenses, and he managed to complete his education without borrowing a dime.

Beth realized Frank couldn't afford much while he was attending college and admired his financial discipline and resourcefulness. While their dates and his gifts to her were inexpensive, they were thoughtful and reflected his deep love for her.

But after they married and both earned a good income, financial conflicts began to develop. Frank insisted from the beginning that all their income go into a bank account that he controlled. He was making a selfish demand.

Beth knew he was a good money manager and he wasn't squandering their income—but he wouldn't tell her how the money was being used. He engaged in the Love Buster dishonesty.

One day she posed an important question. "Frank, do you think we're ready to raise children?"

"Not yet," he replied. "It'll be a while before we can afford them."

Beth bristled. "We can afford children now! We both earn good incomes and we've been saving most of it—haven't we?" Suddenly she felt uncomfortable. "By the way, how much have we saved?"

There was a long pause. "We just haven't saved enough. Take my word for it," Frank said.

His selfish demands and dishonesty were beginning to catch up with him. The next day, when Beth was home alone, she started poking around Frank's papers. What she found blew her away. Frank had all their investments in *his* name. Savings accounts, money market accounts, and stocks—all in his name. The most remarkable part of it was that he had managed to save over twenty-five thousand dollars in just two years!

That evening Beth confronted him with her discovery.

"Why are all our savings in your name? And how can you say we can't afford children when we've saved twenty-five thousand dollars?"

Frank was furious. "I handle all the finances and I do it the way I see fit. Besides, you wouldn't understand it even if I tried to explain it to you. So stay out of my desk!"

Frank may have been *saving* money but he was *losing* love units. Beth was terribly offended and ended the conversation.

The very next day she opened her own checking account. When she was paid, she deposited her check into it.

That evening, Frank said casually, "You haven't given me your check. Do you have it yet?"

"Yes, I do," she said flatly, "and you're not getting it!"

This time *she* lost love units in *his* Love Bank. In fact for the next year, she lost love units each time she deposited her check into her own account. It seemed fair to her, but it annoyed him.

By the time they saw me for marriage counseling, their complaint was that they'd "grown apart." She had her life, and he had his. Their inability to resolve their financial conflict had implications in many other parts of their lives, and their separate checking accounts had begun the process of separating everything!

Their problems began with Frank's selfish demands and dishonesty. He wanted to control the finances and didn't want her to interfere. With incomplete information, Beth gradually suspected that Frank was cheating her.

Frank's motives were pure: He was saving money for both of them and was not trying to cheat her, but his arrogant approach destroyed her trust in him.

Beth contributed to the problem when she set up her own checking account. Even though Frank had been secretive with her about their finances, she should not have made the same mistake. Instead, she should have cooperated with him regarding her finances and complained bitterly about the way he was treating her.

When Beth explained that her discovery of their savings in Frank's name had upset her, he refused to transfer their investments into joint accounts. He knew his actions had been at her emotional expense but did nothing to protect her feelings. If he had simply added her name to all their investments and thoughtfully requested that she deposit her check into a joint account, the issue may have been settled.

Most of us would consider Beth's defensive reaction reasonable under the circumstances. But it turned into a good example of how defensiveness can be thoughtless. Her behavior deeply offended Frank, even though he'd done essentially the same thing to her. If she had not deposited her checks in any account until she'd reached an agreement with Frank, it would have been a thoughtful example to him.

The elimination of Love Busters and the application of the Policy of Joint Agreement solved their problem. Frank agreed to disclose his investment strategy to Beth and added her name to all their investments. At first, he felt offended that she had not trusted him but he came to realize she had a *right* to the information he had kept from her—she had a *right* to discuss all financial planning with him. Besides, it was essential in preserving her feelings of love for him.

They both agreed that from that point on, all financial decisions would be made together, all investments would be made in both of their names, and they would deposit their paychecks into a *joint* checking account. When it came time to pay the bills and decide how much would go to savings, they would both come to an agreement before any checks were written.

Their cooperation in financial matters encouraged a cooperative spirit in other areas of their marriage as well. As time went on, an increasing number of their habits and activities were changed to take each other's feelings into account. They no longer drifted apart because they'd learned how to create compatibility.

They went on to have children, and as far as I know, conflicts in financial planning never again threatened their love for each other.

Married to a Spendthrift

For many of us, spending more money than we have seems to be instinctive. We usually know that at least one of our ancestors was financially undisciplined. We probably inherited the trait from him!

Shirley had inherited the trait in its purest form. From early childhood she could not resist buying things she wanted. Her father had tried to help her control her spending, but she'd become so upset whenever she couldn't have something that he'd finally given in and handed her the money she needed.

While Joe dated her, he bought her things she wanted as gifts, because he enjoyed seeing her reaction: She seemed to live for her next gift from him. Shirley was an attractive woman, and Joe's generosity brought out the best in her and made her appear even more attractive to him. Within six months, they were head over heels in love with each other.

Since Joe was an executive in a growing company, he earned a good living. It never occurred to him that Shirley's buying habits could cost him more than he earned.

In the first few years of their marriage, he justified many of her purchases as necessary for their new home. But soon she wasn't satisfied with her initial purchases and had to buy replacement items. The closets in their home became so filled with her clothes that she gave away many items to make room for a new wardrobe.

Joe became alarmed. "Shirley, I think it's time we discuss something. You're spending more than we can afford."

She became genuinely concerned. "Oh, Joe, are you having financial problems?"

"*We* are having financial problems! My income is better than ever, but you're spending more than I earn," he complained. "We'll have to start a budget so we can keep our expenses under control."

"That's okay with me," she responded cheerfully. "Just give me an allowance each month, and I'll stick to it!"

Joe worked out a budget for Shirley, but in the first month she *didn't* stick to it. When Joe tried to talk to her about it, she shrugged it off as a bad month and promised to do better the next month. But the next month was no better.

Now Joe became upset. "Shirley, are you trying to ruin me? You're spending money I don't have."

Shirley's voice remained calm. "Take it easy, Joe. You must be upset about something that happened at work. I think you're overreacting."

He couldn't hold his anger in any longer. "Overreacting? My problem is that I haven't reacted soon enough. I've got to put an end to this immediately. I'm taking your name off our checking account and canceling all our credit cards. I'm sorry, but it's the only way I can get your irresponsible spending under control!"

Shirley was visibly hurt by his words. She knew her spending was out of control but she felt he had no right to treat her like a child. His angry outburst and selfish demand were easily explained by the circumstances, but they hurt her nonetheless.

His anger had the predictable effect. Shirley ignored his demands. The next time she saw something she wanted to buy, she simply withdrew money from their savings account. Within six months, all their savings were gone.

By the time Joe and Shirley came to my office, Joe was threatening divorce. "How can she say she loves me—and steal me blind? I just can't go on like this."

"I admit I have a problem controlling my spending, but I love Joe and I think he still loves me. He knew I liked to shop before we were married. I'm no different now from how I was then," she said in her defense.

Shirley's excuse that she had a "problem controlling her spending" was nothing more than admitting her selfishness. She knew Joe would be furious when he discovered their savings gone but she cared more about buying that next item than protecting Joe's feelings.

It's important to realize that Shirley really loved Joe. She simply neglected to protect his feelings, and in the process Joe lost much of his love for Shirley.

Through counseling, I was able to convince Joe that Shirley was not doing all of this out of revenge for some unknown childhood experience. She had developed a very thoughtless habit. But that knowledge didn't restore any love units. Shirley had to overcome the habit if the marriage was to be saved.

Joe was on the right track when he tried to negotiate a solution, but when his initial effort failed to change her habit, he should have continued negotiation, perhaps with the help of a marriage counselor.

Over a period of months, Shirley learned to control her spending habits. We used a procedure similar to the one I described in chapter 4 which deals with annoying behavior. Her thoughtless way of buying things for herself was replaced with a thoughtful, mutually acceptable approach. She still did quite a bit of shopping, but the money she spent was well within their budget.

Now that Shirley had learned to take Joe's feelings into account, she wanted to be included in decisions Joe made that affected her. Joe had been accustomed to making decisions for her, and now he faced an adult wife with opinions and feelings that were not always the same as his.

With the gaping hole in his Love Bank repaired, love units that she deposited by meeting his emotional needs quickly restored his feeling of romantic love for her. It helped give him the desire to include her in his decision making, and eventually they learned to accommodate each other's feelings in adult transactions.

What If You're Both Spendthrifts?

Financial problems are at the core of many divorces. This is true because of the way people treat each other when financial disaster looms before them.

Mel and Cindy were a happy-go-lucky couple who never missed an opportunity for a good time. Mel had a decent job but didn't earn nearly enough to support their standard of living. Cindy worked when she felt like it, which wasn't very often. Most of the time, they got along very well but whenever they had a conflict over money, sparks would fly.

Mel had a terrible problem with his self-esteem, and once in a while Cindy would remind him that Nate, a former boyfriend, earned more money than he. To prove to Cindy that she had made the right choice, Mel let her buy whatever she wanted—whether or not they could afford it. From time to time, he explained to Cindy how seriously indebted they were, but it would invariably start a fight, during which she blamed him for failing to earn more.

A point was finally reached where Mel could no longer pay the bills and, without telling Cindy, tried desperately to consolidate them one more time. He believed right up to the end that someone would lend him the necessary money. But one day the sheriff came to his home to serve his wife with a foreclosure notice.

Cindy had a few friends over the morning the sheriff arrived. She was embarrassed beyond words. When Mel came home that evening, he received the tongue-lashing of the century. Within a week, she had kicked him out of the house.

"When you have all this straightened out, you can return home. But until then I don't even want to look at you. You disgust me!"

"Listen to me for just one minute," Mel pleaded. "If it weren't for your reckless spending, we wouldn't be in this mess. I've done the best I can to keep us from bankruptcy, and you just keep spending money as if it's water."

"Don't make excuses for your laziness!" she fired back. "If you had an ounce of ambition, we'd have plenty of money. Get yourself in gear or say good-bye."

Mel came to my office to see if I could help him save his marriage. I arranged for an appointment with Cindy and discovered to my surprise that she was terrified at the prospect of trying to support herself. She was willing to take Mel back only because he was able to earn something, and something was better than nothing. Not a great motive to save a marriage, but I'll usually take anything at first.

Neither of them were taking responsibility for their financial woes, yet they were both to blame. In a way, they had conspired with each other to create the appearance of wealth. Their motives were different, but they both knew what they were doing. They just weren't willing to accept the inevitable consequences.

Many of these situations end in divorce because both husband and wife become vicious in an effort to shift blame to the other. They punish each other so effectively that before long one or both of their Love Bank accounts become overdrawn, and the marriage comes to an end.

Whenever Mel tried to discuss finances with Cindy, they'd have a fight. They tried to blame each other for their problems and then punish each other. Love units evaporated quickly whenever that happened, so they didn't discuss money very often. Angry outbursts and disrespectful judgments were the culprits at this stage of the problem. Because they couldn't control their anger, a thoughtful resolution never got off the ground.

The first step toward reconciliation was learning to control their angry and defensive reactions. I helped them learn not to blame each other but rather assume their share of the responsibility for their problems. Once anger and defensiveness were gone, they could discuss problems intelligently and with consideration for each other's feelings.

Mel and Cindy did lose their house and had to file for bankruptcy. But because they both learned to avoid Love Busters, their marriage survived the ordeal. In a way, the bankruptcy gave their marriage a new start it couldn't have had without a clean financial slate.

With this new start, they learned to share financial information with each other and to make decisions together. Before long they were in a rented home they could afford, and their standard of living kept pace with their income.

I'm almost certain Mel and Cindy will have financial problems again in the future. Almost all married couples do. But when these problems develop, they won't use the destructive methods of the past that withdrew love units. Instead, they'll use thoughtful solutions that help build romantic love.

Deciding between Two Worthy Causes

Both husband and wife often have legitimate positions in a disagreement but they may be poles apart. Helping them decide on a common ground compromise sometimes takes the wisdom of Solomon.

The issue that divided Kevin and Marcia was how to budget their income. Kevin had a good job but he was always afraid he'd be laid off and the family would have nothing to fall back on, so he insisted on putting part of each paycheck in a savings account. Marcia was more confident of Kevin's job security and felt that helping their children pay for college was more important than saving money. Saving part of each paycheck for unforeseen emergencies was a good idea. But helping their children through college was also a good idea. Which idea was better?

Kevin and Marcia came to my office in the hope that I would decide the issue for them. The solution to their problem, of course, was not mine. They had to decide for themselves.

To begin, I explained that whatever they decided had to take each other's feelings into account. They must both be enthusiastic about their final decision. They'd never quite thought in those terms, but it didn't take them long to learn the Policy of Joint Agreement.

I had each explain to the other why his or her position was important. Kevin told Marcia about his fear of losing his job and having difficulty finding another. Having savings that would carry them for a year would make him feel much more secure, since he felt he could be reemployed within that time. She felt the savings would be a waste, since he was already investing in a retirement plan, and the main purpose of a padded savings account would simply be to provide him with an added sense of comfort.

Then Marcia expressed her concern that without financial assistance their children might miss the opportunity to complete a college education. She considered it the obligation of parents to see their children through college. Since Kevin had never attended college, he wasn't as sold on college as a necessary step toward adulthood.

I reminded them that they needed to resolve the conflict with a decision that would take both positions into account. The outcome could not annoy either of them. One solution that would pass that test was to neither save their money nor help their children. (Remember, you have to *do* something annoying to be engaged in an annoying activity. Doing *nothing* may also be annoying but, technically, failure to act doesn't count). They both objected to that solution and immediately set out to come to a compromise.

"How would you feel if . . . ?" took the place of "Stop being so stubborn!" Marcia suggested that she work more and that her salary go to their children's education. When she asked how Kevin felt about that idea, he pointed out that it would take her away from him and that if they gave the kids money for college, he wanted it to come from both of them.

Kevin suggested that he wouldn't object to cosigning student loans. If they had the money later on, they would pay off the loans for their children. When she was asked how she felt about that idea, Marcia explained that she didn't want her children to face life with debts, even if there was the possibility that they would be paid later.

Through their discussion of possibilities, they learned not to challenge each other's feelings. Even when they seemed unbelievable or unreasonable, the feelings were accepted as final. For both of them, this created a much greater willingness to cooperate. They became more and more creative in the discussion and finally arrived at a solution they both liked.

When their negotiations ended, they both agreed that the most important outcome of the discussion was the love they felt for each other. In fact it got to a point where both had reversed their original positions: He was willing to sacrifice his savings for the children's education, and she was willing to use the money for his savings. Since I don't approve of sacrifice as a solution, they continued to negotiate until they both reached an enthusiastic agreement.

Their ultimate compromise was a combination of taking some money from savings (but not enough to make Kevin uncomfortable), and cosigning a student loan that Marcia did not feel would be burdensome. The compromise did not sacrifice love units, and that was the most important outcome.

When budgets are created to benefit one spouse at the expense of the other or when money is spent by one spouse without considering the feelings of the other, love units are lost. It's that simple. A wise financial plan considers the feelings of both spouses, and this helps build romantic love.

Chapter 9 of *His Needs, Her Needs* explains how to make a realistic budget and how to stick to it. If you need help in budgeting your money, I encourage you to read that chapter.

Resolving Conflicts 10
over Children

*G*reg was a single parent of two teenagers, Allan, thirteen, and Vivian, fifteen. The three had a comfortable lifestyle, and Greg tended to spoil his children. Since the death of his wife, eight years earlier, Greg had dated only two women, Bobbi and Janet. He liked them both very much, but Janet enjoyed being with his children, and Bobbi didn't. That single factor caused him to break up with Bobbi and eventually marry Janet.

As soon as they were married, however, conflict developed between Janet and Vivian. Once Janet had moved into their home, Vivian started "borrowing" her clothes without asking. Janet didn't say anything at first, but after her favorite sweater disappeared, she'd had it!

"Vi, have you seen my pink sweater?" she asked.

Vivian didn't miss a beat. "Nope."

"Are you sure?" Janet pressed. "You may have taken it to school and left it there."

"I've never taken any of your sweaters to school! Why would you think I took it?"

"Well, you've taken some of my other clothes, and I thought maybe you'd taken the sweater, too."

"I can't believe this! Look, I haven't taken your sweater. *Okay?*"

There was no way to prove Vivian had worn the sweater, but Janet knew her clothes hadn't sprouted legs. When Greg came home that night, she explained her problem to him. Greg asked Vivian about the sweater. She denied ever wearing it and became angry that they were ganging up on her over something she had nothing to do with.

After that incident, more of Janet's clothes disappeared. One day while Vivian was in school, Janet searched Vivian's room and found almost all her missing clothes. When Greg came home, she told him what she'd found. He confronted Vivian with the evidence. His daughter burst into tears and denied having had any of those clothes in her room. It was her word against Janet's, and she accused Janet of lying. In an effort to calm everyone down, Greg said they'd discuss the matter some other time.

Janet was furious.

Vivian put a lock on her door.

As the months passed, the relationship between Janet and Vivian worsened. When her father was gone, Vivian made rude remarks to Janet and openly challenged her right to live there. Greg tried to stay out of the growing conflict. But one day Janet could take no more.

"Greg, it's either me or Vivian. The two of us can't live in this house together."

Greg was stunned. "What do you want me to do? I can't kick out my own daughter. Besides, she'll only be with us for another three or four years. Can't you hold out that much longer?"

"Yes, Greg, I could. But I won't. It's perfectly clear to me that she comes first in this house, and I'm not living in a home run by a spoiled brat!"

Greg lost control with that remark. "I think we have *two* spoiled brats living in this house. But Vivian's only fifteen! What's your excuse?"

Janet moved out.

In my office, Greg and Janet reviewed their disastrous first year of marriage. Each of them thought it had been a mistake to get married.

But I reminded them that prior to marriage, they were highly compatible and loved each other as much as they had loved anyone. Their loss of love was a direct result of the way they'd handled Vivian. She had come between them. They needed to discover a way to complete the job of raising her without further destroying their love for each other.

In my office, Greg laid his cards on the table. He told Janet he had never punished Vivian for anything. When he knew she had taken Janet's clothes, he didn't know how to respond. So he tried to avoid the issue. He recognized now how much Janet needed him to help her resolve the problem and he apologized for his failure.

I helped Greg and Janet decide how they would handle the situation when Vivian verbally abused Janet or took her clothes. Simply telling Vivian to stop wouldn't work.

Throughout their discussions, they made no demands on each other and agreed they would not settle on a plan that annoyed either of them. The discussion itself was hard on Janet because Greg kept coming up with ideas that favored Vivian. She was hurt by each suggestion. I explained to her that Greg did not intend to hurt her and that the negotiation itself was an opportunity to help him understand her reactions to these alternatives.

I suggested that Janet remain separated from Greg until the solution regarding Vivian's behavior was implemented. For several weeks, they worked out this problem together and eventually agreed on a strategy to overcome it.

Janet admitted that the loss of her sweater was not as painful as the feeling of being abandoned by Greg. He admitted he was in the habit of defending his daughter unconditionally, and it was clearly at Janet's expense. He agreed to consider Janet's feelings first in family decisions, the same way he'd treated his first wife.

This was a significant turning point in their crisis. When Greg agreed that protecting Janet's feelings would be among his highest priorities, the crisis was essentially ended. That was all Janet wanted from him. She knew teenage girls can be hard to handle but she wanted reassurance that as Greg's wife she would come first in his life.

With Janet gone for several weeks, Vivian started feeling guilty about the whole thing. On her own initiative, she invited Janet back to the home but never did admit stealing the sweater. While she didn't take any more clothes from Janet, she was still rude and insulting once in a while.

The next time she offended Janet—and it was within a week of her homecoming—Greg and Janet discussed the problem with Vivian as if it affected them both. He explained to her that whenever she hurt Janet's feelings, she was hurting him too. She had to learn that her dad was now a part of Janet; if she loved him, she needed to care for his new wife.

Each time she offended Janet, Vivian could expect to engage in a discussion with Janet and her dad. Within a year, her rude remarks had all but disappeared.

By teaching his children to be considerate of Janet's feelings, Greg implemented a good childrearing objective, one that helped both children learn to become less self-centered. But something else was far more important: Greg and Janet learned that once they were married, not even his children should come between them.

This example shows how Love Busters can interfere with the solution of a marital problem. Angry outbursts, disrespectful judgments, annoying habits, selfish demands, and dishonesty all contributed to making a wise solution impossible for Greg and Janet to achieve.

Some of the most frustrating and difficult marital problems are found in blended families (where at least one spouse brings children from another marriage into the new marriage). Because couples in blended families are less likely to apply the Policy of Joint Agreement, the rate of divorce in these families is extraordinarily high. But when they apply thoughtfulness, reasonable solutions begin to emerge, and the risk of divorce is eliminated.

From Perfect Lover to Perfect Mother

Wayne had dated many women and was even engaged once, but no one seemed to meet his high standards well enough to make him want to tie the knot—that is, until he met Kris. She was everything he'd always hoped for, and she loved him too. She was absolutely perfect as far as Wayne was concerned.

Those who knew Kris well were not surprised by the good job she did as Wayne's new wife. She had a history of doing things well. Ever since early childhood, she was able to focus her attention on personal objectives and achieve them with excellence, one by one. When she fell in love with Wayne, she wanted nothing more than to be everything he needed in a wife, and she was able to achieve it.

Kris became the perfect lover, meeting all Wayne's known marital needs and some he never knew he had. She was his lover, friend, recreational companion, greatest admirer, and kept herself extraordinarily attractive.

When Rachel, their first child, was born, Kris's focus of attention changed. Now she had a new personal objective: to be the perfect *mother.* At first, Wayne was delighted with the care and attention she gave their daughter. After all, he wanted the very best for Rachel and knew that Kris could provide it.

But after a while it became apparent that Rachel's gain was his loss. Kris couldn't leave Rachel for a moment, and when they were together as a family, Rachel had her mom's undivided attention. Wayne knew that somehow he had to find time alone with Kris.

Walking in the front door one evening, he said, "Hey, hon, let's go to the hockey game tomorrow night. A guy at work has tickets he'll give me."

"No, thanks, not this time," she said pleasantly. "But you go ahead, if you'd like, dear."

"What's gotten into you?" he teased. "You used to *love* the North Stars!"

Kris was not smiling. "We can't go out and have fun and forget about Rachel. She needs as much attention as we can give her. What we do for her now will affect the rest of her life."

"Now wait a minute! I'm talking about one evening out. Surely her whole life won't be ruined if she spends an evening with your parents."

"I *said* I won't go. That's it!" Kris turned and walked out of the room.

Wayne wondered what had happened to his perfect lover. She must have left one day, and her twin sister, the perfect mother, showed up in her place. He did go to the hockey game with a friend at the office. It started a pattern in which he worked late or went out with friends most evenings.

Even though their marriage had started to show signs of decay, Kris insisted on having more children. Over the next seven years, they had three more, and she dedicated herself to their care. They loved her dearly because she not only took responsibility for their training but was cheerful and fun-loving in the way she went about it.

She wished Wayne would take a more active role in raising their children, but when she tried to discuss it with him, he explained that with four children he had to keep his nose to the grindstone to keep up with the bills.

In my last example, Greg had let his daughter from another marriage come between him and Janet. But even when the children are your own, they can easily come between you and your spouse. Kris's effort to give their children the best opportunities in life came at Wayne's expense.

People usually enter marriage with the best intentions to be loving and caring partners in life. But when children arrive, a new ideal—to be loving and caring parents—sometimes conflicts with the ideal of partnership. When that happens, the Policy of Joint Agreement becomes particularly important.

Wayne showed up in my office one day to try to gain perspective on his life. He was falling in love with a woman at work but didn't want to start an affair. Marrying Kris, he thought, had been the biggest mistake of his life. He couldn't go on living this way but didn't know how to change things without filing for divorce.

"All she really wanted was children. I don't think she ever really did want a husband," he told me. "I'm not even sure she loved me. How could I have been so stupid?"

I tried to assure him that Kris had loved him and probably still did. She had simply made a choice between two ideals—being a good lover and being a good mother—and chose one at the expense of the other. She had not grasped the consequences of her shift in emphasis. At the end of our conversation, he was willing to let me speak with her about their marriage.

Kris was upset about the marriage, too. She felt Wayne had abandoned her as soon as their children arrived. When he left her alone so much of the time, it encouraged her to focus on the children even more.

I explained to her that it was in the children's best interest for their parents to be in love. To achieve that objective, their schedules had to take each other's needs and feelings into account. Her schedule took the children's feelings into account, but not Wayne's. His schedule didn't take her feelings into account.

I recommended a plan designed to flush out all the cobwebs: a vacation for just the two of them.

It worked like a miracle. During their vacation together the old Kris returned. Wayne couldn't believe it. He became the center of her attention again, and it brought the best out in him.

When they returned home, I saw them immediately. Habits are often conditioned by environment, and I knew Kris was likely to revert to old habits on her arrival home. Sure enough, as soon as she got home with the children, her twin sister, the perfect mother, arrived!

But they were prepared. They had already agreed on a schedule that would allow them to be together without the children fifteen hours each week. As part of the overall agreement, Wayne scheduled an additional fifteen hours to be with Kris and the children.

At first Wayne didn't think he could find thirty hours to spend alone with Kris and their children. As they discussed his schedule together, he realized that he engaged in numerous activities and interests that did not have Kris's enthusiastic support. Since they'd agreed to apply the Policy of Joint Agreement to all their behavior, he abandoned these activities and interests in favor of those he could share with Kris, and in the end everything fell into place.

They'd made the mistake of failing to take each other's feelings into account. Unilaterally, they created habits and activities that annoyed each other terribly. But they couldn't seem to escape from them because these activities were based on important ideals. Their story illustrates well how ideals can help create Love Busters.

Knowing your spouse is uncomfortable with something you're doing should be enough to encourage you to change your behavior, no matter how right that behavior might seem to you. The Policy of Joint Agreement helps prevent you from using ideals to destroy romantic love.

Three in Bed Is One Too Many

Andre and Patti had a great marriage, and when the kids came along it was still great. But they had one fly in the ointment: Susan, their three-year-old, insisted on sleeping with them at night. At first Andre thought it was cute. But after a while, when Susan became a nightly resident in their bed, he didn't think it was so cute anymore.

"Patti, we've got to do something about Susan sleeping with us," Andre suggested one morning over coffee. "Don't you think we need more privacy?"

"Oh, she'll outgrow it. It's just a phase she's going through," Patti responded.

"Well, it's starting to bother me, and it sure has affected our love life!"

Patti shook her head. "If we tell her she can't sleep with us, she may think we don't love her. We can't do that. Just be patient."

Every once in a while, Andre would raise the issue with Patti. Her response was always the same: She felt it was wrong to create anxiety in Susan by forcing her to sleep in her own room. Besides, whenever they encouraged her to try it, Susan threw a fit.

The problem didn't improve for a solid year, and Andre became more and more upset. Before he asked Patti to help him solve the problem, she hadn't lost too many love units in his Love Bank. But after she told him to just put up with it, he started to blame her for the problem—and love units were withdrawn at a rapid rate.

It never occurred to either of them that Andre's love would be affected by the situation. He only knew his interest in Patti had taken a nosedive. When they came to see me for counseling, he blamed his lack of love on his work, his personality flaws, and possible unconscious negative attitudes toward women. Patti couldn't imagine what his problem was, since she still loved him very much.

An analysis of their marriage identified Susan as the unwitting culprit. In most cases I encourage a husband and wife to come to a joint agreement without my interference. But in this case, Patti wanted my professional opinion regarding Susan's emotional welfare. I suggested that Susan be taught to sleep in her own bed, not only for the sake of the marriage but also because it was healthier for Susan. I suggested that if this habit continued, Susan might grow up emotionally handicapped by an unhealthy dependence.

An even more important consideration was that Patti had given the feelings of her daughter a higher priority than the feelings of her husband. Letting her daughter sleep with them annoyed Andre, yet Patti did nothing to protect him from that annoyance.

The plan for getting Susan back into her own bed worked. And then Andre reported that his love for Patti was being restored. To me, it was a foregone conclusion that as soon as they removed that burr in the saddle, all the great things they'd learned to do for each other prior to Susan's intrusion would take over, and romantic love would be restored.

When Discipline Becomes a Love Buster

Alex had a short fuse. Everyone in his family and all his friends knew it. When he fell in love with Christine, he knew his temper would ruin his chances with her, so he learned to perfectly control it in her presence. He also had the sense to know he should never abuse her after marriage. So he vowed to himself—and to her—that he'd never try to punish her verbally or physically. So far, so good.

However, he was raised in a tradition where heavy-handed discipline was considered a parent's duty. As a child, he'd been beaten on occasion. His parents had explained to him that he was to obey them or expect disastrous consequences. Since no one's perfect, he got the disastrous consequences from time to time.

When their first child arrived, Alex expected the same unwavering obedience that his parents had expected of him, and he disciplined his child the way he had been disciplined. The first time it happened, Christine became very upset and begged him to stop. She consulted with the pastor of their church, but the pastor thought Christine should leave the discipline up to her husband. He gave her examples of children who grew up to be criminals because women raised them without a man's discipline.

The temper Alex had learned to control with Christine he released on his children. Whenever he felt irritated about something, he punished the children more severely. They grew up with considerable fear of him. But all the while he was careful never to treat Christine abusively. In fact he went out of his way to be sure she understood that his punishment of the children was a father's responsibility, something that had to be done.

All his explanations never did change her feelings, however. Every time he punished their children, she suffered. It was as if he were punishing her, and she cried almost every time it happened. Even though he had shown exceptional care for her in other ways, the suffering of their children caused a huge loss of love units from her Love Bank.

Finally, Christine reached the end of her endurance. "Alex, I can't take this anymore," she objected. "I don't care if the children disobey, leave them alone! You're too hard on them."

"We've been through this before. Children will not obey their parents unless they are punished for disobedience. If I stop punishing them, I'll be encouraging them to sin."

"I don't care if they sin. Leave them alone!" she screamed.

Alex looked her right in the eye and said, "Christine, I'm sorry, but you'll have to submit to me as you're commanded to in Scripture."

Christine saw me for counseling the next day. She was referred by her pastor. Alex grudgingly agreed to meet with me the following week.

My appeal was simple. The punishment of his children was also punishment of his wife. She identified with them and suffered when they suffered. I explained that discipline should be a joint decision between husband and wife, if for no other reason than to preserve the couple's love for each other.

I also pointed out that Christine had an important perspective on child rearing that he should consider. A *joint* perspective would benefit their children greatly. It's amazing how much trouble we can avoid by simply making joint decisions with our spouse. We double our wisdom and take so much more into account when the decision is made not to proceed unless both are in agreement.

I gave Alex and Christine a simple assignment: There would be no discipline unless both agreed to it. Alex was not convinced at first that the shift from punishment to a system of rewards that Christine supported would work but he soon discovered that rewards were far more effective in teaching his children good habits. Constant punishment merely created resentment and rebellion.

Alex overcame a most annoying habit that withdrew love units. In the course of thoughtful negotiation, he developed a new habit that deposited love units. Christine needed his involvement in their children's training. When he learned to do it in a way that took her feelings into account, he was able to restore romantic love.

If methods of child rearing are imposed by one spouse without enthusiastic joint agreement, they are almost certain to fail. More important, they are Love Busters. Thoughtfulness in decisions of child rearing is wise and effective. Children clearly gain when both parents can agree on how they're to be raised. This eliminates confusion from mixed messages and stupid, emotional, and impulsive decisions made by one spouse in the heat of anger.

Children can come between a husband and wife, destroying their love for each other. In most cases, it isn't the children's fault, but rather one or both parents, who assign a higher priority to the care of their children than they do to the care of each other. Only when spouses make each other's feelings their highest priority can children be successfully integrated into a family without the loss of love. For further reading on this subject, see chapter 11 in *His Needs, Her Needs.*

Resolving Conflicts 11
over Sex

Kathleen was a very attractive woman. To be more precise, she was an absolute knockout!

Jeffrey was one of the only men she'd dated who was more interested in her intelligence than her body. In fact they spent their first date discussing how to help the handicapped, one of her greatest concerns. Since they both majored in social work, they shared many of the same values. For hours they discussed the problems of society, and he consistently expressed compassion for the under-privileged. He also had a profound respect for women, which Kathleen appreciated.

Even though she had made love to some of her past boyfriends and usually enjoyed it, Kathleen had felt guilty and sometimes used. When she explained these feelings to Jeffrey, he suggested they wait until marriage to make love. At first, she thought his suggestion was too impractical—but it got her attention and impressed her! She interpreted his patience as respect for her and a willingness to place

159

her feelings above his selfish desires. He earned hundreds of love units for that "selfless" attitude.

After graduating from college, they were married, and on their wedding night Kathleen looked forward to making love, having waited for two years. But Jeffrey was too tired! Kathleen was crushed and cried most of the night.

The next morning, however, they made love for the first time. Kathleen was visibly disappointed. Jeffrey ejaculated after less than a minute of intercourse.

Kathleen wanted to try again that afternoon, but again Jeffrey was too tired. And that evening he was still too tired. From the beginning to the end of their two-week honeymoon, they made love only five times, and each time it lasted only a few minutes. Kathleen must have tried to get him interested fifty times! It was a frustrating start to her marriage, and she lost her temper. In fact she threatened to get an annulment if he couldn't get his act together.

But Jeffrey did everything else right. He was a great conversationalist, was affectionate and considerate, and made her the center of his life. She couldn't have asked for anything more—except sex!

"What's the matter with you?" she blurted out shortly after they arrived home.

"What do you mean?" he asked.

"Do you realize that when a woman is sexually rejected by her husband it makes her feel unattractive? Maybe I'm not your type!"

"Oh, no, Kathleen, you're the most beautiful woman I've ever seen."

With that he gave her a big hug and tried to make love to her. He made a real effort to improve his sexual responsiveness, but within three months he found he could no longer have an erection when they tried to have intercourse.

"What does this mean, Jeffrey? You really don't find me attractive, do you? All the time I thought you were treating me with respect, you were simply uninterested! Why did you marry me, if you didn't find me sexually attractive?"

"You are sexually attractive, believe me. I simply have a problem expressing it. I want to make love to you, but my body doesn't cooperate!"

"You're not telling me the truth," she pressed. "You must think I'm a fool! If I were attractive to you, your body would work just fine."

At our first interview I discovered that Jeffrey was more sexually frustrated than Kathleen. He needed a good sexual relationship, but the pressure she put on him to perform had made him afraid to have sex with her, and it had eroded her account in his Love Bank.

He sat bewildered, telling me how preposterous his situation was. She was, indeed, very attractive, and most men would consider her the sexual fantasy of all time. But here he was, unable to respond and finding himself becoming unwilling to respond.

In almost all marriages one spouse is more ignorant of sex than the other. Usually it's the woman, but in Jeffrey and Kathleen's marriage, it was Jeffrey. He had postponed sex until marriage, a commendable goal. But that decision left him sexually inexperienced. Since his sexually experienced wife knew considerably more about it than he, he felt intimidated.

When they first made love, all his worst fears were realized! He completely lost confidence in himself. After their first month of marriage, he had been raked over the coals so many times that he had started to develop a strong aversion to having sex with Kathleen. From there, it was a short trip to impotence.

Kathleen ridiculed Jeffrey's sexual performance because she thought he was lazy and needed pushing. Besides, it made her angry, and she felt better after she let him have it!

I commended them both for having the courage to seek professional help for a sexual problem but explained that no marital conflict is resolved through punishment or ridicule. Angry outbursts and disrespectful judgments don't bring solutions closer; they drive them away.

Once Kathleen realized that Jeffrey's sexual problem did not mean that he didn't find her attractive but reflected his inexperience, she made a commitment not to ridicule Jeffrey for sexual failure. That crucial first step provided the opportunity for a solution to be implemented.

The assignment I gave them—a common approach to impotence—was for him to take sexual initiative. He was also able to explain to Kathleen what she did to make sex unpleasant for him, and she made a few important changes in her method of lovemaking. Kathleen was to expect no sexual fulfillment for herself until they completed this assignment. He learned to maintain an erection without ejaculation while having intercourse.

When the woman has problems with sexual responsiveness, the solution is essentially the same with reversed roles: The man is to expect no sexual fulfillment, and his wife learns how to become sexually aroused by taking initiative. Her husband follows her instructions, and he learns from her how to make love to her.

Kathleen had sexual techniques in mind that had to be abandoned when they discussed the effects they had on Jeffrey. She also wanted him to engage in sexual marathons from time to time, and for Jeffrey these were worse than Chinese water torture. By the time they got it all sorted out, they not only made love several times each week, but they found it mutually fulfilling.

When Kathleen stopped making disrespectful judgments and selfish demands on Jeffrey, it provided an opportunity for Jeffrey to become sexually proficient. As he became more and more experienced, he not only provided Kathleen with greater sexual pleasure, but he also enjoyed their lovemaking more than ever before.

An individual's sex drive is directly related to the ease with which he or she engages in sex. The more one enjoys it, the greater the drive becomes.

Think about that the next time you make love to your spouse. If your spouse enjoys the experience, it will contribute to his or her sex drive. But if you do something to make the sexual experience unpleasant, it will lower your partner's sex drive.

Jeffrey and Kathleen developed excellent sexual compatibility partly because they learned to avoid Love Busters. But they also found it necessary to receive professional help in developing sexual skills.

After you and your spouse have exhausted solutions that you've jointly discussed, you may need to consult a professional sex therapist for solutions you've not yet considered. Many methods have been developed to help couples overcome sexual incompatibility, and you should try each of them until you find one that works for you.

Does Sin Make Sex Painful?

Nicole was born out of wedlock, and her mother never married. In fact her mother had sex only once in her lifetime—when Nicole was conceived. That single sexual encounter had been extremely painful, and she felt certain it was God's punishment for her indiscretion.

She told her daughter that God often punishes women by making sex painful and that if she ever married she should expect pain while having intercourse.

Nicole married Doug, a quiet, hardworking farmer. They didn't make love prior to marriage, but on their honeymoon her first sexual experience was as painful as she had ever imagined. In fact it brought her to tears. Doug didn't know what to make of it and figured that whatever it was, it would go away. He tried making love to her several times on their honeymoon, and each time she ended up crying.

Remembering her mother's prediction, Nicole simply expected to experience pain every time she made love. Over the next few weeks the pain not only remained intense, but the opening to the vagina eventually closed each time they attempted intercourse. It became impossible for Doug to penetrate. Nicole thought it was God's punishment for her mother's sin, carried over to her. Doug thought it was her way of keeping him from having sex with her.

After the first few weeks of marriage, they attempted intercourse about once a year, but to no avail. On their fifth anniversary, he informed her that he was considering a divorce. That brought them to me for counseling.

They were both incredibly naive about sex. Nicole had been warned by her mother that God punishes sexual impropriety, so she had never engaged in any sexual experimentation. Doug had learned to mas-turbate but had no other sexual experiences prior to marriage. He felt that reading books on sex was a form of perversion. Coming to a counselor was clearly an act of desperation for both of them.

I assured them that if they followed my instructions completely, their problems would be over within three months. It actually took less than six weeks.

Nicole had a condition called vaginismus, in which a muscle spasm closes the opening to the vagina. It's usually caused by tears in mus-cle tissue somewhere in the reproductive tract or a vaginal infection. It has nothing to do with sin.

I explained to her that her mother probably had the same condi-tion when she made love her first and only time. Not knowing what to make of it, she passed it off as punishment.

I had Nicole see a gynecologist first to be certain she was free of infection and had a normal-sized vagina. Sometimes an abnormally small vagina can cause the same symptoms and can be corrected with surgery. The report came back showing that all was normal.

Then she and her husband completed a series of exercises designed to desensitize the vaginal opening so that the muscle spasm was elim-inated. It's a common procedure known by qualified sex therapists. The exercises were carried out daily (a very important part of the assignment), and within three weeks they were gingerly having inter-course. She was completely cured within six weeks and experienced a climax for the first time in her life.

This opened up a whole new world to Nicole and she couldn't understand why Doug didn't want to make love at every opportu-nity—at least twice a day! Doug had to explain to her that he didn't enjoy making love twice a day, and she'd have to settle for three to four times a week. By their last appointment, they had made a good sexual adjustment to each other.

This case is a good example of how failing to take feelings into account can cause physical problems as well as the loss of love units. When Doug tried to make love to Nicole, knowing she was experi-encing pain, he made her physical problem worse. He tried to force his penis into her, and then once inside he used quick strokes that were not only extremely painful but also strengthened the painful reflex.

The solution to the problem of vaginismus was a procedure that simply required a very slow and painless penetration of the vagina, enough stimulation to be felt but not enough to cause pain. Over time the speed of penetration was increased, but slowly enough to be painless. The reflex eventually disappeared entirely.

If Doug had simply insisted on painless penetration when he made love to Nicole using plenty of lubrication and going very slowly, he would have followed the correct procedure on his own. Thoughtfulness solves most of our problems in life.

If you ever do something sexually that causes your spouse to experience physical or emotional pain, you may lose more than love units. You may contribute to physical and emotional problems that your spouse may find very difficult to overcome.

Solutions to sexual problems follow the Policy of Joint Agreement. The procedure leading to a resolution of the problem must be mutually agreeable and enjoyable. When you're both happy making love, you're on the way to resolving sexual problems. In a sense, you've already resolved them.

Don't Wait Until It's Almost Too Late

Throughout their long marriage, Grace and Ben had been known for the affection and consideration they showed each other. No one, including Grace, imagined the seriousness of their marital problem.

From their first anniversary on, Ben had expressed his deepest love for his beautiful and charming wife. But on their fiftieth wedding anniversary, an occasion for special appreciation for a happy and fulfilling marriage, he gave her a card that said, "Thanks for ruining my life!"

Grace thought she was having a nightmare. It was totally unexpected, and she cried for days. Ben felt ashamed and begged her forgiveness. But the cat was out of the bag.

When she finally gained enough composure to discuss the matter with him, Grace wanted him to explain himself. "Ben, this is the tenth time I've asked you this, and I expect an answer. What did I do that ruined your life?"

"Please believe me," he pleaded. "I don't know what got into me. You haven't done anything. It's all my fault."

"What's all your fault?"

"Oh, it's nothing. Please forgive me for wrecking our anniversary." He insisted, "I'm just an old fool."

"What is this all about? I will not let you sleep until you tell me, so you may as well tell me now and get it over with."

"Okay," he agreed, "but remember, it's not your fault! I know you've never experienced a climax and sometimes I feel I've missed out on something that's very important to me. That's all."

"Ben, I don't know how."

"Don't worry about it." He shrugged. "We're too old to do anything about it now anyway."

Throughout their marriage, Grace had not put much effort into sex. At first she didn't think it was all that important. But when it became apparent that Ben enjoyed it, she went through the motions just to make him happy. She always thought that someday she'd learn what it was all about.

It never occurred to her that *her* pleasure was an essential part of sex and that Ben couldn't be sexually fulfilled unless she experienced arousal and climax with him.

But she took a very important step that day. She decided to get help and made her first appointment with me that week.

I suggested she bring her husband with her next time and had them read the book *Woman's Orgasm: A Guide to Sexual Satisfaction* by Georgia Kline-Graber and Benjamin Graber (New York: Warner Books, 1975). The book not only showed her how to climax but also how to climax during intercourse, a difficult achievement for most women. They worked daily on the prescribed exercises and had never had so much fun with each other.

Grace learned how to climax and was happy that Ben had brought the problem to her attention. Her regret and his was that Ben had waited so long to tell her how much it bothered him. If he had told her early in their marriage, she would have done something about the problem. The solution would not only have helped Ben, it would have revealed to her how enjoyable sex can be.

The Love Buster that prevented their sexual fulfillment was dishonesty. Ben failed to communicate his frustration until it was almost too late. Although he used an angry outburst to communicate his problem, the revealed truth was more constructive than the anger was destructive. Grace recovered from the pain quickly because it was so out of character for Ben. In other words, his angry message was not a habit but rather a single act for which he later apologized.

When Grace discovered the problem, she eagerly set out to solve it. To a large extent, her love for Ben made it rather simple to learn to climax. She trusted him completely and felt safe and relaxed in his company. The quality of their relationship made the solution easy.

We're all wired right; it's just a matter of learning where the controls are. If you're a woman who isn't sure you've ever experienced a climax or if you climax very seldom, get a copy of the book I mentioned above or some other book explaining how women can experience a climax. If you go through the recommended exercises and still can't quite get it, consider the help of an experienced sex therapist.

An effective sex therapist usually won't mind if your husband is part of each counseling session. It should be up to you. All exercises should be done in the privacy of your own home, either alone or with your husband. A therapist should never touch you or have you experience any form of sexual arousal in the office. Therapy for most sex-related marital problems is completed within three months and is sometimes covered by health insurance.

If you're at all uncomfortable with one therapist, go to another. Your gynecologist should be able to recommend several, and you may wish to consult with two or three before you settle on one.

Sex Should Be Shared

Whenever a client tells me her husband is impotent, I'm a little suspicious. While I've treated many men who were truly impotent, more often than not the problem turns out not to be impotence at all, but rather excessive masturbation.

I once counseled a man who brought himself to ten climaxes each day. By the time his wife wanted to make love, he was sexually exhausted! When he stopped masturbating, he had absolutely no problem at all making love to her.

But that wasn't Jerry's problem. He could do both. If Jane, his wife, ever wanted to make love, he was ready and able. He initiated lovemaking on a regular basis himself. But every once in a while she would discover evidence that he'd been masturbating. It made her furious—so much so that she made an appointment for marriage counseling.

When Jerry discussed the problem with me, he couldn't understand why she was upset. "Why should she care if I masturbate? We make love whenever she wants, don't we? And I'm an excellent lover besides. What's her problem?"

Jane had explained to him that she wanted all of his sexual feelings to be directed toward her. She felt that his masturbation was like a mistress, and she didn't want to share his sexual feelings with a fantasy.

I explained to him that whenever he masturbated, he was doing something that he enjoyed but that she hated. Her alternative suggestion wasn't unreasonable either: She was willing to make love to him anytime he wanted.

Then came the real dilemma. He confessed that he enjoyed masturbation more than he enjoyed sex with his wife. He wasn't sure if he could stop.

Masturbation had become such a pleasurable experience for him that sex with his wife was sometimes boring in contrast. He made love to her out of duty and did a good job of it but he looked forward to masturbating more than anything else. He felt that since no other woman was involved it was okay for him to develop a sexual procedure that brought him so much pleasure.

But he actually *had* another lover: himself! Jane had good reason to feel jealous. Some of the effects of an affair were developing in his marriage: He was robbing his wife of some of the very best feelings he could have toward her, sexual feelings. All those love units that could have been deposited in her account were squandered.

I also advised him that many men with sexual perversions—such as making obscene telephone calls and exposing themselves in public—started with an effective program of masturbation. Perversions are usually avoided when a man brings his wife into his sexual experiences and limits his sexual activities to those they mutually enjoy.

I recommended to him that if at all possible, sexual feelings be reserved for marital lovemaking. He should avoid sexual fantasies if they didn't involve his wife, he should avoid sexual arousal if his wife were not present, and he should most certainly never experience a climax unless it was while making love to his wife.

In this case my recommendations were followed, and Jerry was able to overcome his habit of masturbating. He knew this Love Buster offended Jane but he had done it anyway because he enjoyed it. In other words, he gained at her expense. When he decided to protect her feelings, he stopped masturbating. It also may have prevented him from developing an embarrassing and potentially career-threatening sexual perversion. But most important, it helped build romantic love for both of them.

Sex is a tool that helps bring a man and a woman together in marriage but can actually drive them apart when it is given a status higher than that of the marriage itself or when it is overlooked and ignored. Without a good sexual relationship, a marriage is usually in serious trouble. All married couples need to develop the skills that will help them provide sexual fulfillment for each other.

BONUS
CHAPTERS

Building Romantic Love 12
with Care

When Jo and Pete married, the most clearly understood part of their wedding vow was that they would care for each other throughout their lifetime. They understood that care means more than a feeling, it's a commitment to make every reasonable effort to meet each other's needs.

While they were still dating, Pete told Jo that if she married him he'd make her the happiest woman in history. She'd be the center of his life, and his world would revolve around her. Jo knew that if the marriage was to work she had to treat him the same way. She had to make him happy as well and make every effort to meet his needs.

While they each had the right intentions and the correct understanding of care as a marital commitment, they did not understand how difficult it would be to *learn* to care for each other. They both thought care was something you could decide to do, and once the decision was made, acts of care would be spontaneous.

But because their care for each other was not carefully planned, it fell far short of expectations. Both Jo and Pete felt neglected.

Care is the *willingness* to change your own personal habits to meet the emotional needs of the person you have chosen to marry and then *making sure* that those habits are effective.

Care does not cause anyone to lose his or her identity or to become a robot. Our habits are very often developed through chance and are not necessarily a reflection of our character or our major goals in life. When we change them to accommodate our spouse's needs, we are actually controlling our behavior to fit our character.

But the process of discarding old habits and developing new ones is difficult and stressful. This is one reason well-intentioned couples often fail in their efforts to learn more accommodating habits. It's not only difficult for us to change for our spouse, but it is also difficult to put our spouse through the stress of making changes to accommodate us.

Jo and Pete thought they were compatible when they were married. They got along with each other extremely well and felt that they were made for each other. It did not occur to them that after marriage new marital needs would develop and prior acts of care would slowly fade away.

Care is more than learning to meet another's needs at a point in time and sustaining those habits; it also requires the willingness and ability to meet changing needs—adjusting to a moving target.

One of the more popular reasons for divorce today is that a husband and wife have "grown apart from each other." One of them may have completed an education, while the other did not. One may have developed a new career interest, and the other did not join in that interest. Very often children impact a couple's interests and send them in different directions.

I believe that one reason couples grow apart is that they fail to care for each other. Instead of learning how to meet each other's needs, couples assume that their instincts will carry them. Then when instinct seems to fail, they conclude that they must be incompatible. Growing apart means that a couple has not grown in compatibility. They have let nature take its course, and the new needs that are inevitable in marriage are left unmet, because no effort has been made to create new habits to meet them.

Extramarital affairs and multiple marriages represent one strategy in adjusting to the failure to create compatibility. Over a period of time, as needs change and a relationship falls apart, a new relationship is developed with another individual who, by chance, is prepared to meet those new needs.

If we were unable to adjust to each other's changes in life, then I suppose multiple marriages would be about the only solution to satisfactory relationships. But we have an enormous capacity for adjustment. Learning to meet each other's marital needs is far less complicated than going through the agonizing ritual of divorce and remarriage.

Step 1: Discover Your Spouse's Most Important Needs

The first step in learning to care for your spouse is discovering his or her emotional needs and identifying the most important ones.

Men and women often have very different marital needs—especially the most important ones—and this makes discovering your spouse's needs complex and difficult. Because men try to meet needs most important to men and women try to meet needs most important to women, a couple can easily become confused and fail to meet each other's real needs.

When the best efforts of a man and woman go unappreciated and their own needs are not met besides, they often give up trying. If they had only directed their efforts in the right places, they would have been effective and appreciated.

My experience as a marriage counselor has pointed out ten of the most important emotional needs that can be met in marriage. While all ten are important, five are of critical importance to most men, and the other five are of critical importance to most women. All these categories may not apply to your marriage, but they can help you begin a discussion with your spouse to identify the needs you should learn to meet.

A man's five most important needs in marriage tend to be:

1. *Sexual fulfillment.* His wife meets this need by becoming a terrific sexual partner. She studies her own sexual response to recognize and understand what brings out the best in her; then she shares this information with him, and together they learn to have a sexual relationship that both find repeatedly satisfying and enjoyable.

2. *Recreational companionship.* She develops an interest in the recreational activities he enjoys most and tries to become proficient at them. If she finds she cannot enjoy them, she encourages him to consider other activities that they can enjoy together. She becomes his favorite recreational companion, and he associates her with his most enjoyable moments of relaxation.

3. *Physical attractiveness.* She keeps herself physically fit with diet and exercise, and she wears her hair, makeup, and clothes in a way that he finds attractive and tasteful. He is attracted to her in private and proud of her in public.

4. *Domestic support.* She creates a home that offers him a refuge from the stresses of life. She manages household responsibilities in a way that encourages him to spend time at home enjoying his family.

5. *Admiration.* She understands and appreciates him more than anyone else. She reminds him of his value and achievements and helps him maintain self-confidence. She avoids criticizing him. She is proud of him, not out of duty, but from a profound respect for the man she chose to marry.

When a man is married to a woman who has learned to meet these needs, he'll find her irresistible. Love units are deposited into his Love Bank in such great numbers that he finds himself helplessly in love. That's because the fulfillment of these needs is essential to his happiness.

A woman's five most important needs in marriage tend to be:

1. *Affection.* Her husband tells her that he loves her with words, cards, flowers, gifts, and common courtesies. He hugs and kisses her many times each day, creating an environment of affection that clearly and repeatedly expresses his love for her.
2. *Conversation.* He sets aside time every day to talk to her. They may talk about events in their lives, their children, their feelings, or their plans. But whatever the topic, she enjoys the conversation because it is never judgmental and always informative and constructive. She talks to him as much as she would like, and he responds with interest. He is never too busy "to just talk."
3. *Honesty and openness.* He tells her everything about himself, leaving nothing out that might later surprise her. He describes his positive and negative feelings, events of his past, his daily schedule, and his plans for the future. He never leaves her with a false impression and is truthful about his thoughts, feelings, intentions, and behavior.
4. *Financial support.* He assumes the responsibility to house, feed, and clothe his family. If his income is insufficient to provide essential support, he resolves the problem by upgrading his skills to increase his salary. He does not work long hours, keeping himself from his wife and family, but is able to provide necessary support by working a forty- to forty-five-hour week. While he encourages his wife to pursue a career, he does not depend on her salary for family living expenses.
5. *Family commitment.* He commits sufficient time and energy to the moral and educational development of the children. He reads to them, engages in sports with them, and takes them on frequent outings. He reads books and attends lectures with his wife on the subject of child development so that they will do a good job training their children. He and his wife discuss training methods and objectives until they agree. He does not proceed with any plan of training or discipline without her

approval. He recognizes that his care of the children is critically important to her.

When a woman is married to a man who has learned to meet these needs, she'll find him irresistible. Love units are deposited in her Love Bank in such great numbers that she finds herself helplessly in love. That's because the fulfillment of these needs is essential to her happiness.

Of course, *these categories do not apply to everyone.* Some men look at my "man's needs" list and throw two out to make room for two from my "woman's needs" list. Some women do the same. Believing that these categories are right for everyone is a big mistake!

I suggest these needs to help a couple start the process of identifying what they need the most in marriage. It is simply a way of helping you think through what makes you the happiest and most fulfilled. I also want couples to realize that what a man needs in marriage is usually quite different from what a woman needs. That makes the whole process of discovering your needs very personal; it's something you must do for yourself. Then you should explain your discovery to your spouse.

To make this process more accurate and reliable, I suggest that you first pick one need from the ten. Pretend that, in your marriage, it's all you'll get. The other nine needs will *not* be met. What need would you pick if you knew you would never get the rest? That's need number one.

Then do the same for need number two. If you will *not* get the other eight needs met, what two would you pick? Continue this process until you've picked five. Those are likely to be the needs you want your spouse to focus primary attention on.

Take a hard look at the needs you left behind. For example, if you did not include financial support, you should not expect your spouse to earn a dime! Are the needs you chose more important to you? How about physical attractiveness? If your spouse neglects her appearance, gains weight, or dresses carelessly, what would your emotional reaction be?

Some of my clients tell me that all ten are of critical importance. They could not survive a marriage that neglected any of them. But my experience has shown me that if you can learn to do an outstanding job meeting only the *five* most important needs, you build more romantic love than if you do a mediocre job on all ten.

Most of us cannot be outstanding at everything; we must pick what is most important and concentrate on that. If you want to build romantic love with your spouse, meeting the *most important* emotional needs will do it.

Once you and your spouse have communicated your five most important emotional needs to each other, you're ready for the second step in learning to care for each other.

Step 2: Learn to Meet Your Spouse's Most Important Needs

Learning to meet your spouse's five most important marital needs usually requires literally hundreds, maybe thousands of new habits. But the habits all eventually come together to form a whole. It's like learning a part in a play: You begin by learning each line, each motion, each cue, but eventually it comes together. It's naturally whole; it doesn't seem like hundreds of little pieces.

To build the myriad of habits necessary to meet your spouse's needs, you must have a carefully planned strategy. *His Needs, Her Needs* provides a few strategies for you to consider for each of the ten needs. But the need for financial support may require you to consult a vocational counselor. The need for sexual fulfillment may require help from a sex therapist.

However you develop it, a strategy—a plan—should be created that has a good chance of improving your ability to meet the needs your spouse identified as most important.

Once you implement your plan, you may need someone to report to for accountability. Your spouse is not a good choice, because your mentor may need to criticize your effort, and your spouse should not be forced into that role. A pastor or professional counselor may be better suited.

Finally, when you have completed your plan, your spouse is the ultimate evaluator of success. If, after all your effort, your spouse's needs are not being met, you must go back to the drawing board and plan a new strategy.

Honesty is essential at this stage of the program. If your plan does not meet your spouse's needs, it does neither of you any good to claim success.

But if you are successful, your spouse will tell you. You will see it in his or her eyes, and in the way your partner talks to you and responds to you. The "look of love" is unmistakable.

I view marriage as a profession. The skills I learn are designed to meet my spouse's most important emotional needs, and if I'm successful, she'll be in love with me. If she's not in love with me, I'm probably at fault and need to develop new skills. Of course, if I'm not in love with her and I've been honest about my feelings, it's her problem to solve.

As I've said earlier, *compatibility is created.* As a couple increases the number of habits that meet each other's marital needs, it improves their compatibility and their romantic love for each other.

We have such an opportunity in marriage to give each other exactly what we need. Many couples squander that. Don't let it happen to you!

Building Romantic Love   13
with Time

Before Jen and David were married, they spent the majority of their free time together. Her girlfriends knew that spending time with David was one of her highest priorities. Whenever they invited her somewhere, she would first check to see if she'd be missing an opportunity to be with David. Her girlfriends thought it was silly. On some occasions, she even broke dates with her girlfriends if David had time to be with her.

David did the same. Soon he found that many of the things he enjoyed doing were abandoned because he was spending so much time with Jen.

They tried to see each other on a daily basis. On days when they couldn't get together, they called each other and sometimes talked for hours. When they were together, they gave each other lots of attention.

The total amount of time spent with each other in an average week was fifteen to twenty-five hours. This included time on the telephone. But they weren't counting. They just took advantage of every opportunity.

After they were married, however, a change took place in the quality of their time together. They were with each other much more often but they actually spent less time giving each other attention. David came home and watched television all evening. Sometimes he barely said a word to Jen.

Before they were married, they scheduled time to be with each other. But after marriage, they felt that "dates" were not as important, so their time together was incidental to other priorities.

Courtship is a custom that gives people a chance to prove they can meet each other's marital needs. If enough love units are deposited, marriage usually follows. Without time together, the test would fail because it takes time to deposit enough love units to create romantic love.

As a reminder to couples who tend to neglect spending time together, I've suggested the following:

The Rule of Time

Give undivided attention to your spouse a minimum of fifteen hours each week, meeting his or her most important emotional needs.

One difficult aspect of marriage counseling is scheduling time for it. The counselor must work evenings and weekends because most couples will not give up work to make their appointments. Then the counselor must schedule around a host of evening and weekend activities that take the husband and wife in opposite directions.

Another difficult aspect of marriage counseling is arranging time for the couple to be together to carry out their first assignment. Many couples think that a counselor will solve their problems with a weekly conversation in his office. It doesn't occur to them that it's what they do after they leave the office that saves their marriage. To accomplish anything, they must reserve time to be together. This may be painful but eventually they get the point and little by little they rearrange their lives to include each other.

It's incredible how many couples have tried to talk me out of the Rule of Time. They begin by trying to convince me that it's impossible. Then they go on to the argument that it's impractical. Then they try to show me that it's impractical for *them*. But in the end, they usually agree that without time they cannot possibly achieve romantic love.

To help me explain how the Rule of Time is to be applied in marriage, I've broken it down into three parts: privacy, objectives, and amount.

1. *Privacy: The time you plan to be together should not include children, relatives, or friends. Establish privacy so that you are able to give each other undivided attention.*

Why be alone? When you're alone as a couple, you have an opportunity to deposit many love units in each other's Love Bank. When you're with others, everyone gets a little credit. Without privacy, romance in marriage simply comes to a halt.

First, I recommend that couples learn to be without their children during these fifteen hours. I'm amazed at how difficult an assignment that is for some people. They don't regard their children as company! To them, an evening with their children is *privacy.* They think that the presence of their children prevents only lovemaking and they can do that after they go to bed. I think the presence of children prevents much more than that: Children keep the couple from focusing attention on each other, something desperately needed in marriage.

Second, I recommend that a couple learn not to include friends and relatives in the fifteen hours of time together. This may mean there's no time left over for friends and relatives. If that's the case, you're too busy, but at least you haven't sacrificed romance.

Third, I teach couples what giving undivided attention means. Remember, it's what you did when you were dating. There's no way you would have married if you had ignored each other on dates. You looked at each other when you were talking, you were interested in the conversation, and there was little to distract you. This is the undivided attention you must give each other as a married couple.

When you see a movie, the time you're watching it doesn't count because you're not giving each other undivided attention. It's the same with television or sporting events. You should engage in these recreational activities, but your time together is to be very clearly defined: It's the time you pay close attention to each other.

Now that you're alone with each other, what should you do with this time? The second part of the Rule of Time deals with objectives.

2. Objectives. During this time, create activities that will meet your most important emotional needs: Affection, sexual fulfillment, conversation, and recreational companionship.

Romance for most men is sex and recreation; for women it's affection and conversation. When all four come together, men and women alike call it romance. That makes these categories somewhat inseparable. My advice is to combine them all, if you can, whenever you're alone with each other. That's what people do when they write romantic novels or are having an affair. Why limit romance to novels and affairs?

Now for the final part of the rule. How *much* time do you need?

3. Amount: Choose a number of hours that reflects the quality of your marriage. If your marriage is satisfying to you and your spouse, plan fifteen hours. But if you suffer marital dissatisfaction, plan thirty hours each week or more, until marital satisfaction is achieved. Keep a permanent record of your time together.

How much time do you need to sustain romance? Believe it or not, there really is an answer to this question, and it depends on the health of a marriage. If a couple is deeply in love with each other and finds that their marital needs are being met, I have found that about fifteen hours each week of undivided attention is usually enough to sustain a romantic marriage. It is probably the least amount of time necessary. When a marriage is this healthy, either it's a new marriage or the couple has already been spending fifteen hours a week alone with each other.

When I apply the fifteen-hour principle to marriages, I usually recommend that the time be evenly distributed through the week, two to three hours each day. When time must be bunched up, all hours on the weekend, good results are not as predictable. People seem to need intimacy almost on a daily basis.

For couples on the verge of divorce or entangled in an affair, I recommend much more time. In some cases, I have advised couples to take a leave of absence from work and other responsibilities, go on a vacation, and spend the entire time restoring intimacy that had been lost over the years. In many cases, two or three weeks of undivided attention bring a couple to a point where they begin to consider remaining married. I usually counsel them long-distance during this time.

The vacation doesn't usually build enough love units to re-create the feeling of love. But the feeling of hatred is reduced and sometimes eliminated. Remember, in bad marriages, Love Busters have created Love Bank balances that are in the *red*. Negative accounts must first be brought to zero before positive accounts can be built. These vacations are designed to speed up the love unit deposits before the relationship is bankrupt and divorce inevitable.

When marriages are unhealthy but not on the verge of divorce, I recommend an intermediate amount of time together, somewhere between twenty and thirty hours a week. Without the crisis of divorce at hand, I usually have great difficulty talking people into being alone together for this much time.

It's always been a mystery to me how workaholic businessmen find time to have an affair. The man who can't be home for dinner is scheduling mid-afternoon adventures three times a week. How does he get his work done? The answer, of course, is that he had the time all along. It's simply a matter of priorities. He could just as easily have taken time to be with his wife. Then he would have been madly in love with her instead of his secretary.

The reasons I have so much difficulty getting couples to spend time alone together is that they're not in love. Their relationship doesn't do anything for them, and the time spent together seems a total waste at first. But with that time they can learn to re-create the romantic experiences that first brought them together in a love relationship. Without that time, they have little hope of restoring the love they once had for each other.

Whether your marriage needs fifteen hours a week or more than that, remember that the time spent is only equivalent to a part-time job. It isn't time you don't have; it's time you've filled with something less important.

To help couples get into the habit of scheduling time alone, I have encouraged them to make a chart, keeping track of the number of hours alone each week. Each person independently estimates the time actually spent giving undivided attention, and the number entered on the chart should be the lower of the two estimates.

This chart becomes an excellent predictor of marital fulfillment. It's like the Index of Leading Economic Indicators for marital health. During periods when a couple spends a large number of hours alone together, they can look forward in future months to a very warm and intimate love relationship. But when the chart shows that very few hours have been spent together, the couple can expect to find themselves arguing more often and feeling less fulfilled in the months ahead.

I also encourage both husband and wife to carry an appointment book. Here they write down the time they've set aside to be with each other. While I'm counseling them, I make certain that they keep the dates they set for each other and that they are always recorded.

Since we are creatures of habit, I recommend that the hours spent alone be at the same time each day and the same time week after week. You will probably be able to schedule more time together on the weekends. If you keep the same schedule every week, it will be easier to follow the Rule of Time than if you change it every week.

Remember, the total amount of time you spend together doesn't necessarily affect the way you feel about each other in the week that the time was spent. It has more effect on the way you're *going to feel* about each other in future weeks. You're building Love Bank accounts when you spend time together, and the account must build before you feel the effect.

From my perspective as a marriage counselor, the time you spend alone with each other is the most valuable of your week. It's the time when you are depositing the most love units and ensuring romantic love for your marriage.

Willard F. Harley, Jr., Ph.D., is a clinical psychologist and marriage counselor. Over the past twenty-five years he has helped thousands of couples overcome marital conflict and restore their love for each other. His innovative counseling methods are described in the books and articles he writes. One of his books, *His Needs, Her Needs,* has been a best-seller since it was published in 1986 and has been translated into German, French, Dutch, and Chinese. Dr. Harley also leads training workshops for couples and marriage counselors and has appeared on hundreds of radio and television programs.

Willard Harley and Joyce, his wife of more than thirty years, live in White Bear Lake, Minnesota. They are parents of two married children who are also marriage counselors.

Be sure to visit Dr. Harley's web site at
http://www.marriagebuilders.com